This composite portrait of Joyce Grenfell has been compiled by her husband and her editor from the memories of those who knew her and from writings of her own – autobiographical sketches, poems, essays and one or two monologues – that have not been included in her other books.

This entertaining and heart-warming book will be welcomed by all who loved her books, her performances and the woman herself.

Other books by Joyce Grenfell

Edited by
Reggie Grenfell
and Richard Garnett

Joyce by herself and her friends

Futura
Macdonald & Co
London & Sydney

A Futura Book

First published in Great Britain in 1980 by
Macmillan London Limited

First Futura edition 1981
Reprinted 1982

Contributions by Joyce and Reggie Grenfell © The Joyce
Grenfell Memorial Trust 1980

ISBN 0 7088 2078 6

Reproduced, printed and bound in Great Britain by
Hazell Watson & Viney Ltd, Aylesbury, Bucks

Futura Publications
A Division of
Macdonald & Co (Publishers) Ltd
Holywell House
Worship Street
London EC2A 2EN

To
The Reverend Geoffrey Howard White

If I should go before the rest of you
Break not a flower nor inscribe a stone,
Nor when I'm gone speak in a Sunday voice
But be the usual selves that I have known.
      Weep if you must,
      Parting is hell,
      But life goes on,
      So sing as well.

Joyce Grenfell
(date unknown)

Contents

CONTENTS

Foreword

This book is an attempt, in the spirit of Joyce's poem, to compile a portrait of her from the memories of those who knew her, and from writings of her own which have not been included in her autobiographies. Some of these may seem not strictly autobiographical, but everything she wrote reveals her character. We have had to cut our coat to suit our cloth. Fortunately there have been some happy finds among Joyce's papers; and while her own recollections are chiefly of her childhood, most of the memoirs by others describe her in her maturity, so it has not been too difficult to achieve a reasonably balanced picture.

We should like to thank all the contributors to this book, particularly for having written at very short notice.

We should also like to acknowledge our indebtedness to the publications in which some of the contributions in this book first appeared:

The Observer – 'Child by the Sea'; *The Chelsea Society Annual Report* 1979 – 'A Chelsea Childhood' and 'Citizen of Chelsea'; *Nanny Says* (Dennis Dobson) – 'Nannies'; *Everywoman* – 'Small Fry'; *Housewife* – 'The Grenfell Experience', reprinted by permission of A D. Peters & Co. Ltd; *Country Life* – 'Craftsmanship'; The Poetry Society (broadsheets) – 'Sonnet'; *Punch* – 'Lunchtime Concert'; *The Sunday Times* – 'A Civilised Woman'; *The Bookseller* – part of 'A Very Satisfactory Author'; *More From Ten to Eight on Radio Four* (B.B.C. Publications) – 'Wishes for a Godchild'; *Catholic Life* – 'My Way of Prayer'.

If we have overlooked the publication of any other writings included here, we offer our apologies to those concerned.

REGGIE GRENFELL

RICHARD GARNETT

Joyce Grenfell died on 30 November 1979.

A Thanksgiving Service was held at Westminster Abbey on 7 February 1980.

Afterwards the *Guardian* wrote:

Well over an hour before the service was due to begin there were queues outside the Abbey.

'This is rather like a service for a Prime Minister,' said the bewildered correspondent of an American newspaper. 'Joyce was a wonderful woman, of course, but she wasn't Prime Minister, was she?'

In a congregation of 2,000, with 1,500 reserved seats snapped up as soon as they were offered, her fans obviously thought that she was a lot more than a Prime Minister, and perhaps they may even have been right.

REGGIE GRENFELL
Dear Mr Grenfell

It was only after Joyce died that I discovered how many friends she had. Besides all those I knew, there were others with whom she kept up a regular correspondence, sometimes without ever meeting them. (Katharine Moore, who has contributed to this book, is the most remarkable of these.) There were hundreds more who were only wanting the opportunity to become friends. Here are a few extracts from some of the very many letters I have received:

I remember reading once something by David Hockney, who when he heard the news that Picasso was dead went to Christopher Isherwood and said, 'Picasso has died.' Isherwood said, 'Oh has he? That's not like him.' I think Joyce would have liked that said about her.

One evening, when we had supper together, Joyce in the very kindest, gentlest way laid it on the table and made it clear to me that I was living a second-hand kind of life, and that I needed to take a look at myself and work out my own destiny and find the way I should go in the future. I have always been profoundly grateful to her and completely devoted to her, following her advice to break away from the theatrical world. Since then I have served in the Foreign Office and latterly become a priest, very happily married with a large family.

While reading *In Pleasant Places* it struck me that when most people write their autobiographies the unmentionables they leave out are either illegal or immoral (or both). But Joyce's secrets were her generosity and helpfulness to people. The only story she told in her book of giving a present was a back-fire one – Mr Clews's drip-dry shirt.

Your wife meant so much to us who never even knew her. It seemed only appropriate that one very special day when I was going to meet the man I loved – and we both realised it for the first time – on the car radio I heard Joyce singing 'I'm going to see you today'; it seemed right that she was there at a very important moment in my life.

An insurance man came to see us, and suddenly he started talking about the news of Joyce's death. Almost bewildered he said, 'My wife and I always felt better after we'd watched her.' Isn't that the essence of it?

I knew Pips when she was a small guide in the 7th Westminsters.

I never knew your wife, but whenever I heard her on radio or saw her on TV I always thought that she knew me – and loved me.

My husband and I arrived at the Abbey at about 3.30 and joined a queue. I asked a lady in the queue if she knew Mrs Grenfell. She replied, 'No, but I liked her very much. She made me laugh, and I thought I'd like to give her thanks.' We had seats in the North Transept. I said to the man sitting next to me, 'What a lovely tribute to Mrs Grenfell!' He said, 'Yes.' He had come from Durham for the service. 'You know, I'm rather sentimental,' he added. I said, 'Me too.' After the service, when the crowds were going through the main door, a man said to me, 'I knew her.' He'd had lovely letters from her which he would never part with. He and his wife had come from Cumbria for the service. On St James's Underground Station a lady waiting for her train spoke to me and said, 'I see you have been to the Abbey,' because I had the leaflet in my hand, as she also had. I asked her if she knew Mrs Grenfell. She told me she had stayed in the same hotel as Mrs Grenfell in the South of France, and Mrs Grenfell had given her some instructions about the route to take, which she had found easily. She told me she had come from Gloucester for the service. I thought you might like to know this. I would also like you to know I have thought of you both warmly and often, and I always shall.

My 84-year-old Ma said afterwards, 'It's such a mistake when people don't have memorial services. Everyone enjoys them so much.' Then she added, 'I haven't had such a nice day for ages.'

After we left the Abbey we decided to walk through the rain alongside the river to get tea at the Festival Theatre café. It was dusk by then, and suddenly, in spite of the noise of traffic over the bridge, I thought I heard a bird singing. As we came nearer, it was a thrush in full voice singing from the top of a low tree, and incredibly another thrush was singing in the distance like an answering call. I thought how much it would have touched Joyce Grenfell.

TOMMY PHIPPS
My Sister

Looking back on it now I can clearly see that when Joyce peered into my pram (I was two, she was four) and, for no apparent reason, deliberately took a sharp nip out of my nose, I should have realised, there and then, that I had a fairly spiky and rather unusual sister. After all, according to my doting mother, I was pink and white and utterly adorable, and here was this older girl snapping at me like a terrier – and for what? Certainly I'd done nothing to her. In fact, it has been reliably reported that at the time of the attack I was actually sleeping.

It wasn't until I was about five that the truth finally began to dawn. She'd nipped me all right, there was no question about that, but she hadn't done it to be cruel or mean. It was simply her not very subtle way of putting me into the picture. And the picture was that she, Joyce Irene Phipps, was The Boss, that she wasn't going to put up with any nonsense, and that if we were ever going to establish any kind of working relationship for the future I might as well understand, right from the start, exactly how things stood.

Well, I need hardly add, not only did I understand – I never stopped understanding.

To Joyce, from that moment on, I was always the young, lighthearted dilettante, and she was the heavyweight. And, of course, how right she was! In many ways I think Joyce put my mother and me in the same general category. Amusing but hopeless. We might consider ourselves gay and irresistible, but if for a single moment we thought we were going to get away with anything, at least when she was around, we'd better forget it.

My first memory of how taut a ship Joyce was going to run

came about when she and my mother came to visit me at my private school. There had been some late-evening event – fireworks, perhaps – and walking back across the playing-field my mother took the hand of a fat nine-year-old boy called Hardy. They were talking animatedly when Joyce suddenly spotted them.

'Mummy,' she cried, and I can still hear the outrage in her voice. 'Please! Behave yourself!'

And that's the way it was to be for the next fifty years. My mother and I acting foolishly, and Joyce, in the corner, watching us like a hawk.

I think my mother was actually more scared of Joyce than I was. She wouldn't even dare light a cigarette in front of her. My awe took a slightly different form. All I wanted was her approval. My greatest desire was to have her think, despite the overwhelming evidence to the contrary, that I was serious-minded. I can remember so clearly stifling yawns after a late night at the Café de Paris, struggling to make intelligent comments about the affairs of the day.

Of course I never fooled her for an instant. Just the same I wish I'd been aware then of what I was later, that despite her obvious intense disapproval of my endless comings and goings, my outrageous flirtations, my thoughtless extravagances, my quite ridiculously wrong set of values, Joyce, despite herself, was secretly fascinated by what I'd been up to. It was a life she knew absolutely nothing about. Fast cars – cocktail-parties – rendezvous with actresses! It's hard to believe now, but when she found out I'd had a drink with Tallulah Bankhead, she didn't speak to me for a week. And once when I went dancing with Joan Crawford I thought she was going to change her name. But, as I say, in the end her natural curiosity would always get the better of her, and eventually, through clenched teeth, hating herself for doing it, she'd manage a strangled 'Well, go on, Tommy. I know you want to talk about it. What happened?'

But when I was halfway through, the highlights covered, I'd be cut off with a 'How disgusting! What frightful people!'

I never really knew why, when she was young, Joyce was so intolerant. I think perhaps she got a little mixed-up about my father's high standards. She admired him for them tremendously, but for a long time I think she felt you couldn't maintain them and still recognise there was a world which operated without them. Later, of course, whatever had confused her disappeared, and she became not only extremely tolerant, but extraordinarily understanding of the most worldly situations and relationships. But there's no denying that when we were growing up Joyce was inflexible, opinionated and, as far as I was concerned, downright prim.

I will never forget her during the summers when we would go to various small resorts in France. I was forever falling desperately in love with girls called Monique and Jacqueline (there was even a Fifi in there somewhere), and it used to drive Joyce crazy.

She thought there was something silly and faintly indecent about it, and she was always taking me for long walks on the beach and plaintively enquiring, 'Why do you have to spend so much time in the dunes? Why on earth can't you play more tennis?'

I suppose, at the time, this sisterly interference must have been quite annoying, but looking back on it now I see how curiously comforting it was to have someone of more or less my own age who really cared about how I behaved and what was to become of me. But most disturbing and, in a strange way, most challenging of all, was to have someone in your life whom you could never fool. With my father and mother I could get away – at least I thought I could get away – with almost anything. But with Joyce – nothing. She was on to me from the day I was born.

It's interesting to realise that in those growing-up days Joyce was rarely the 'life of the party'. She was, in fact, usually on the sidelines, as often as not by herself, not missing a trick. I knew about this because on the way home in the taxi she'd give a report like a seasoned detective. She knew exactly what everyone had worn, what they'd eaten, whom they sat next to. She knew what music had been played, she knew who had been flirting, who had been bored. She'd describe, with the eye of a portrait-painter, the face of the butler, the jewellery of the hostess, the funny moustache of the violinist, and if there had been a conjuror she'd have had definite ideas of where the rabbit had come from. Not only did she remember everything she'd seen, but also everything she'd heard, and she would regale whoever had come to pick us up with snatches of dialogue until finally she was bustled into her bedroom and the door firmly closed. Even then I would often hear her through the wall, talking to herself, mimicking the voices of the people she'd seen, until my father would come up the stairs, open the door and say, as gruffly as he could ever say anything, 'Joyce. Goodnight.'

Sometimes, if she was really wound up, she'd still go on in a low whisper, and I'd have to sit up in my bed with my ear pressed to the wall. Obviously, during those days of our child-hood, her imagination was working, but it wasn't always evident.

We used to have large family Sunday lunches with my grand-mother. Afterwards, some of us would go for a walk. I was about ten, I suppose, and my cousin and I always walked ahead. For some reason, on one particular Sunday, he and I decided to let off imaginary carrier pigeons. This entailed raising our arms and then flinging them into the air, releasing the pigeons to carry some highly important message to Buckingham Palace or to 10 Downing Street. We'd been doing this happily for some time, when I suddenly felt a sharp tap on the shoulder. I turned to find Joyce glaring at me.

'What on earth do you think you're doing?' she said.

I mumbled something rather lamely about pigeons.

'Pigeons,' she hissed. 'Rubbish! You're just showing off. So stop it.'

Well, of course, we did. Immediately. But for once we got the better of her, because after that we let the pigeons off from under our coats, with just a tiny flick of the wrist.

Joyce wrote about our mother being a fabulous story-teller.

She was. Spell-binding. I can see the three of us now, sitting on the sofa in the studio at St Leonard's Terrace after tea, while my mother wove fantastic, dramatic, mysterious, funny stories about the many different characters she'd created for us. Joyce used to sit quietly, often expressionless. I was far more responsive, laughing, crying, urging my mother on and on. I remember it sometimes made me rather sad that Joyce seemed to get so little out of these glorious moments.

I shouldn't have worried. Fifty years later Joyce remembered every detail.

Some of my aunts and uncles and cousins have often told me that when Joyce was growing up they all sensed her talent. I don't believe it. Oh, she did like to dance, by herself I mean, galloping around and around to the gramophone, her skirts tucked into what I remember were bulging, black knickers. She sang with my mother, learnt poetry with my father. She loved dressing-up, and she adored reading. She didn't just lose herself in a book, she sank into it up to her neck. If ever I wanted to attract her attention when she was into a real winner I simply had to hit her. I remember one particular book, her favourite for a whole summer. It was called *The Head Girl's Difficulties*, and my father sent her into an absolute rage by insisting on calling it *The Dead Girl's Hifficulties*.

When she was young Joyce was not what you might call an expert at laughing at herself. That came later.

I have trouble trying to remember Joyce as a schoolgirl. I can feel her more than I can see her. I know she had a complete lack of affectation. She had the gift of becoming totally absorbed in whatever she was doing: piano-lessons – sewing – the first struggles with a paint-brush – the animated, intense, completely unselfconscious conversations with made-up characters. She was disarmingly, often embarrassingly honest.

'Why do you talk so funny, Mr Abbott?'

'Joyce! Please!'

'But, Mummy, he does.'

'I st-st-st-stutter, my dear.'

'Oh, I say. Bad luck.'

Joyce was never gregarious. She had her very special 'best friends', but with most children she was always rather reserved – private. I rather liked that. It seemed sort of grown-up and interesting.

I don't remember her spending much time in front of the mirror. I suppose she must have gone through a clothes-conscious, prettifying, hair-fixing phase. Living with my mother I don't see how she could have helped it. But whether she did or not, it never mattered, because when we went to children's parties, and later to coming-out parties and balls, I was always secretly extremely proud of the way she'd walk in, her head high, her back ramrod straight. Her dresses, even then, were rather grand and theatrical, and, of course, topping everything off, were those enormous, spectacularly beautiful, all-seeing eyes.

We used to stay at parties quite late because we both loved to dance. Joyce, who did not perhaps look entirely like a feather, did dance like one. We must have covered a hundred miles together, with Joyce knowing the words to every song, and giving me my own private concert.

After she was married, I used to watch her waltzing with Reggie. Other couples used to move to the side. It must have been her first experience of show-stopping. I was particularly nonchalant in pointing out our relationship.

I think it is fair to say that Joyce was really rather a slow starter. But it is easy to see now that the years when she didn't seem to have much direction were the years of her apprenticeship, the years when she was quietly, without fanfare, known only to herself, sharpening her tools.

Where did the talent come from? A perfect mix: half father, half mother. Each on its own not wholly effective, but blended – a knock-out: unbeatable.

I've always thought that Joyce felt more secure with her Phipps blood. Some of her Langhorne blood seemed to make her a bit apprehensive. She was never quite sure where it was going to lead her. It fascinated her, but she distrusted it. She needn't have, because it turned out to be her greatest ally.

There's no question that Joyce did act governessy to me, but, by golly, if anyone else ever showed the slightest criticism, she was on to them like a tigress. Joyce was, without doubt, the world's most family-loving person. An unshakable rock of loyalty.

But of all the memories of our growing up together, I think the strongest is of how very much we all laughed together – and equally well I remember the tears. Our mother throve on drama. She never received a telephone call that wasn't fraught with emotion. Either she'd forgotten a luncheon date (tears), she hadn't paid a bill (tears), or someone's feelings had been hurt (double tears). For us, a family evening at home that didn't end either in hysterical laughter or near tragedy was unheard of.

It seemed to me then that sometimes Joyce remained slightly less involved than my mother and father and I, but now, looking back on it, I can see that what I took to be indifference was actually intense caring. About things that really mattered to her Joyce had no light touch. Our father, by far the greatest influence in her life, instilled in her such a strong sense of responsibility, of duty, that she took her role as a daughter and as a sister with the deepest seriousness.

As I write these words I can see her so very clearly reading my school reports, frowning at the low marks, a sudden beam if, miraculously, she found the slightest word of encouragement. And how proud she was if I ever had any success at games.

Sometimes she would introduce me as 'Tommy', but when she said 'my brother' my day was made.

JOYCE GRENFELL
Child by the Sea

There are two special kinds of light that were particularly potent to me when I was a child: the unexpected brightness coupled with silence that we awoke to after snow had fallen in the night; and the dazzling, salt-smelling wonder of seaside light. (I know that light doesn't smell but the combination of ozone and sun-haze made a whole.)

The first brightness was exciting, because, for a London child, it was rare; but the second dazzle was expected and looked forward to. My young brother and I waited for it in our railway carriage as we puffed along the branch line on the Kentish coast in a soot-smelling slow-stopping train. In my selective memory it was always fair weather for the journey. A derelict windmill was the sign I always looked for. When it came into view we got down from the string-mesh rack our buckets and spades and my shrimping net. It meant that, any minute now, over rolling fields of long grasses blowing in the inevitable seaside breeze, we would have our first sight of the amazing sea. There, where we had left it a year ago, was the dreamed of pale blue sea. The sea – the SEA!

My brother Tommy was too small to go shrimping. I was eight and full to bursting with anticipation of a repeat pattern of previous times by the sea – all the scents, the feeling of rough stones under the soles of my thin sand-shoes as we picked our way from the top of the beach, safely through sharp sea-grasses that pricked my bare legs, to the soft white sand. There I took off my sand-shoes and felt the first remembered pleasure of cool sand between my toes. Then I ran, lurching through the soft sand to the hard-packed proper beach-sand, damp from the outgoing tide. And stood and sighed with satisfaction. It was as good as I had remembered.

Our beach made a long shallow curve that ended in a rise of distant cliffs five miles away. The land between was flat and treeless, good for golf courses. I never bothered to find out what went on around the corner nearest to us at our end of the curve. It was enough to have all that glorious space to move and play in. I never met a cave or a rock-pool until I was grown up so I didn't know what I was missing. I was quite satisfied with space that included driftwood, seaweed and shells. For colour there were yellow sea-poppies with holly-like grey leaves, sea-pinks and white sea-campion. Treasures included salt-encrusted bottles and the odd shoe or two. There was never a sign of plastic.

When I was a child we didn't know the freedom of near-nudity and the feeling of sun and salt air on the skin, for we didn't strip off on the beach except to bathe. A small girl wore a cotton vest, a strange contrivance misnamed a Liberty bodice, petticoat (sometimes two, one flannel, one cotton) and knickers under her cotton frock. Before I was allowed to paddle and dig canals I had to put on paddling drawers. These were bib-fronted voluminous rubber knickers into which my skirt and petticoat were stuffed. This produced a pantaloon look and was uncomfortable. Since it was all part of sea-side life I didn't mind the rubbery smell.

Because of the extra strong ultra-violet rays beside the sea it was decreed that all children should wear hats. Mine was made of white cotton and was tethered by elastic under the chin. This, too, was uncomfortable because the elastic was too tight and caused me to tickle; but we were told not to fuss and didn't for long.

At low tide some of the older children rode bicycles on the sands showing off to each other: 'Look – no hands!' They made fancy turns on the splendid and endless beach, leaving clover-leaf tracks to prove their skill. Being London children we didn't have bicycles, but our country cousins, who were our hosts by the sea, sometimes allowed us to have a wobble on their bikes. The tentative track-marks I made were pitiful.

But most of the time was spent by all of us, as it has always been spent by young children on beaches, in building and knocking down bucket-pies and sand-castles. We made channels for the incoming tide to run up in order to undermine the turreted and pointed constructions that we had purposely built for such destruction. We also took it in turn to bury each other in the drier sand at the top of the beach. I never quite liked the increasing weight of sand as I was well interred. On the days when my father joined us we buried him too. A huge task.

None of us was allowed to bathe until two hours after our last meal. We donned our unisex, one-piece bathing dresses, dark blue, bordered at the neck and around armholes in white that soon went blue as the dye ran after contact with salt water. At first I wore a bath cap with a frill, very cissy it was, but as I graduated from squealing in the shallow waves to swimming a little with one foot on the bottom I was given a red rubber bathing cap that folded flat like a forage cap. It was hell to put on because the rubber was stiff and to do the job efficiently it had to fit tightly. Mine pulled up my eyebrows into a position of surprise. It too smelt powerfully of rubber.

Our time in the water was strictly controlled. Some of us tended to turn blue if left in too long. Not me; I like cold water and am a glower, but I, too, had to come out when summoned. 'Come on out ... You've had enough.' I hadn't, but it was no good arguing. What I have never cared for about bathing in Britain is the walk back from the water to where the bathing towels have been left, for all too often there is a nippy breeze.

Even as a child I was a people-watcher and I spent happy times on the beach watching and inventing stories for myself about the families I saw. Sometimes, bravely, I spoke to other little girls who, like me, were shell collecting. (Boys collected seaweed ropes, dead crabs and starfishes; they also splashed us when we were all in the sea together. They didn't, then, appeal to me.) 'Have you found any cowrie shells?' was a useful opener.

Cowries were the most prized shells on our beach. We put our heads together to inspect each other's findings, and thus beach-friendship began. 'What's your name?' 'How old are you?' 'Will you be here tomorrow?' 'Oh, good.'

There were no ice-cream vendors, no donkeys or Punch and Judy shows on our beach. But we drew enormous pictures with the points of our metal spades on the hard sand. It was a status symbol of maturity to have a metal spade. We long-jumped, ran races, played rounders (reluctantly in my case, I was not much good at rounders). And we sat for ages smoothing the sand on either side of where we had settled, and after a time I wandered off with my new beach-friend. 'Don't go too far – we'll be going home soon.'

Sometimes I feel that beaches need people to complete them, but not always, and never too many at a time. Almost empty beaches with at most two or three family groups of all ages, a couple of young people in love enjoying the space – that's about right.

Whenever I now find myself on a beach I go on people-watching and in particular it is children-watching that is the most rewarding. The very small child who isn't quite sure he likes the sea but can't resist going towards it, runs unsteadily into the first wavelet – turns to see whether there is help at hand 'just in case' – laughs, half-glee, half-doubt – runs back from the incoming foam-edged spread of water. Does this over and over again, liking it better, until he dares to stand still and allow the wave to break over his brown toes. It is a moment of triumph.

I once watched a little boy about four years old, absorbed in examining a razor shell, first from a standing position from whence it had caught his eye. Then he crouched down to look at it more closely; picked it up and finally, with it in his hand, he stood up still regarding it with intense concentration. Then he flung it away.

During the war I had some leave from my job and I went up to North Wales. Sand dunes and miles and miles of yellow sands were a good antidote to entertaining in hospital wards. One hazy afternoon of a still, golden day I watched a little girl, evidently new to the sea, making discoveries. This is what I wrote about her:

> About three, I suppose,
> On the very edge of the pale grey sea,
> Jumping flat-footed for splashes
> On each little curling wave,
> And laughing with ecstasy.
> Starfish hands stiff with excitement,
> Limp silk hair blowing across her eyes
> Unnoticed; all the world lost.
> Her bathing drawers (courtesy garment)
> Are damp and long about her thighs,
> The small brown body naked to the skies.
> Complete absorption in the task at hand:
> To jump on every curling wave
> Just as it breaks upon the sand.
>
> 'Coo-ee, come back. It's time for tea.'
> No response,
> Only a new interest:
> Stones for throwing at the sea.

JOYCE GRENFELL

A Chelsea Childhood

Most of my long life has been lived in the Borough. I am a Chelsea pensioner, with a small p. I don't wear a handsome scarlet coat, but for practically all of my youth and until six years after my marriage I lived within sight of the Royal Hospital. During the 1914–18 war my family had a first-floor corner flat, number 8, in Burton Court, Franklin's Row. Then in 1919 we moved over to the north side of Burton Court to number 28 St Leonard's Terrace, one of the two five-storey houses of the earlier period; the ones with front and back gardens. Panelling in the tiny vestibule at 28 was said to date from the eighteenth century, although the studio it led into was a more recent addition and had been built on to the house by a horse painter, whose four-legged models came in through a gate at the end of the back-garden leading from Woodfall Street. They were led up a ramp into the studio. By the time we arrived the stable-door end of the long room had gone, and so had the skylight. A tall window, curtained in lipstick-red silk, with a matching cushioned window-seat, made an attractive improvement to a room for living in. Woodfall Street was then still in use as a mews, although most of the stables had been turned into garages.

For some reason (a sense of defeat?) the strip of gravel at the back of 28, overgrown with sooty privet, ground-elder and some non-flowering lilac bushes, was not made into a garden. This was before the Clean Air Bill; Lot's Road power station gushed out plenty of visible pollution. The place was dirty and uninviting, and we seldom played there. But the many children living in Woodfall Street played – noisily – the other side of our garden wall, over which with monotonous frequency bounced their rubber balls. It was usually little boys who had to walk round, via Smith Street and then along the Terrace, to ring our front door-bell to ask for their return. Sometimes little girls came to ask for a hoop or a battered doll that had somehow flown over the dividing wall. My mother once answered the door-bell and found two diminutive games-players standing on the door-step. The older of the two jerked his thumb at the younger and said: 'This yere bloke's lost 'is borl.' The bloke was at most four years old. It was a nuisance having to go out into the sooty bushes to look for whatever had been lost, and I am not sure that the household always acceded to requests. I know I was often the one who had to do the unwanted searching job, and I can't say that I always did it entirely with grace.

One of the blessings that that suspect word 'progress' has brought about – anyway in London – is the disappearance of the very under-privileged look. When I was growing up, in the 1920s, there were still Dickensian conditions to be found even in a modestly well-to-do neighbourhood like S.W.3. The big money preferred Belgravia and South Kensington, and of course Mayfair. Chelsea continued to be a 'them-and-us' society, and children living less than fifty yards from our house were sadly seen to be both ill-dressed and under-nourished. Thanks to St Michael and other merciful levellers, this is no longer evident.

Just round the corner from St Leonard's Terrace two of the larger houses in Smith Street, on the left going towards King's Road, were hostels. 'Beds for Men', it said on the brass plate. On warm-weather evenings residents could be seen, through opened uncurtained windows, lying on thin-looking iron bedsteads. Further along Smith Street another, smaller, quieter house was a Shelter for Fallen Girls. I don't think it had a brass plate, and if it had it would not have put it quite as bluntly as that, but I knew it was a place I was not to ask too many questions about. The gloomy beige rep half-curtains hid from my nosey gaze the sight of anyone, fallen or upright. I don't remember seeing anyone go in or out of the little house. I always hurried by Beds for Men but was less apprehensive about the Fallen Girls.

My parents were not well-off. There was often a faint *crise* at the beginning of the month when bills came in, but they managed to employ a cook-general, a house-parlour-maid, and, to look after my brother and me, there was a much-loved nanny. Every morning during the week tradesmen called at the back door for orders. I remember a special friend from the village-like grocer's shop that stood, where there is now a furrier, between Smith Street and Wellington Square. The shop smelt as such places should of bacon, spices and freshly-ground coffee. Orders were written in a little book and delivered within an hour. The same service came from the butcher, greengrocer, and the fishmonger, who also sent round big blocks of ice, to be housed in primitive zinc-lined ice-boxes, to keep fresh the perishable foods. Milk came in great highly polished brass churns mounted on a hand cart, and was ladled into customers' own jugs. There was seldom room to store them in the ice-box, so the jugs, covered in dampened butter-muslin or coarse crocheted nets edged with blue beads, stood in cool corners, often on the window-sill of the semi-basement kitchen. In summer butter was seldom very firm.

Our newspapers and stamps came from a little newsagent-cum-post office in the middle of the block now occupied by Safeways. It was run by another agreeable friend and his smiling wife. They reserved copies of *Puck* and *Rainbow* for me, and when bills came to my parents they were headed 'Sidney Smith, Lieut.'.

I described some of these things in a book of memories, *Joyce Grenfell Requests the Pleasure*, published in 1976, but I don't think I wrote about the taxi-rank and cabmen's shelter that stood in Royal Hospital Road and could be seen across the cricket ground, in Burton Court, directly opposite our windows. I even remember its telephone number, though I'm not sure of the exchange; I believe it was Sloane, and the number was certainly 2525. When my mother, a lavish user of taxis, lifted the ear-piece and spoke the number into the daffodil-shaped instrument, the girl at the exchange put her through at once;

and we could watch the cab-driver come out of the little dark green shelter, shaped like a land-fast Noah's Ark, get into his taxi and hurry round to our front door. It seemed there was always a cab on the rank when we needed it. In the twenties, and well into the thirties too, there was also always a policeman on his beat patrolling our area. We got to know our guardians of the peace, and as a small child I was taught to greet them as friends and allies. I was comforted by their presence, particularly at week-ends when the pub in Smith Street closed down, and sounds of song and unnerving expressions of exuberance reached me up in my little bedroom on the fourth floor of number 28.

Another amenity that worked splendidly was the postal service. There were at least five deliveries a day, two before midday, three during the afternoon and evening. The clang of the heavy metal door of the pillar-box (no longer on the corner of the Terrace and Smith Street) rang out about 11 p.m. and signalled the last collection of mail. A letter posted before 9 a.m. was delivered in London the same evening. Stamps for a letter cost a penny; postcards and unsealed envelopes went for ½d. Telegrams were cheap. I think we paid 1s. 6d. (about 7½p.) for twelve words and they arrived quickly after dispatch.

Eccentrics have always been part of the Chelsea scene, and as children we were fascinated by the bizarre characters we came to know by sight, in particular the pretty, but sad, lady in black with a chalk-white make-up and flowing black draperies over her picture-hat. And there was the Jesus-man with his long golden hair and unnaturally pink-and-white complexion. He looked like a sentimental illustration in the New Testament; it was rumoured that he was an artist's model and posed for religious pictures. In those days artists really did look like artists in books. We marked them down by their wide-brimmed black felt hats and flowing ties. Some of them even wore velveteen jackets.

We often saw Augustus John, not only in the King's Road and down by 'The Blue Cockatoo' on the Embankment, but also having his luncheon in Queen's Restaurant just off Sloane

Square in Cliveden Place. Epstein and his wife with her straight-cut black fringe, and Laura Knight in a feminine version of the black felt hats were also familiar sights. Their fame added colour to our lives, and at that time they seemed like giants.

While we were still living in Burton Court I went to a small dame school kept by Miss Berman, who was a very small dame indeed – at most five foot tall. This was at number 35 (or was it 36?) St Leonard's Terrace, one of the later houses at the Tedworth Square end of the street. When we moved on to 28 I went to another school, the Francis Holland in Graham Terrace, where I stayed until I was fourteen and went away to boarding-school.

As little children we had taken our picnic-tea into Ranelagh Gardens, the eastern part of the Royal Hospital grounds, but after the move to St Leonard's Terrace there was no longer time for such frivolities. It was in the same grounds that the Chelsea Flower Show and the Theatrical Garden Party were held; both were important events in my youthful calendar. I still enjoy the Flower Show, but the Garden Party no longer exists.

From my nursery window in the corner of our Burton Court flat we had a perfect view of the crowds coming and going from these occasions. As well as making an early visit to the Flower Show with my parents I often went again with my nanny later in the week, on the last day when plants and cut flowers were sold off cheaply. We staggered home with booty for our 'garden', a three-foot-long twelve-inch deep balcony ledge outside the French window in the nursery. But between the ages of ten and fourteen *the* big day for me was the Theatrical Garden Party. I had been stage struck since I'd first been taken to a theatre, aged seven, to see a war-time revue at the Hippodrome.

My parents knew many people on the stage, and my mother escorted me to Ranelagh Gardens – me panting with anticipation – to spend my shillings and sixpences, at stalls run by her friends, in aid of the Actors' Orphanage. The great names of the era were Gladys Cooper, Fay Compton, Noël Coward, Gerald du Maurier, Owen Nares, Ivor Novello, Gertrude

Lawrence; and of course Chelsea's own Sybil Thorndike, Lewis Casson, Nicholas Hannen and Athene Seyler. These stars presided over side-shows and took part in brief entertainments in big marquees. One of the shows was called The Grand Giggle, and with like-minded little friends, as steeped in star-worship as I was, I queued for ages to see my favourites. No teenager today, with a screaming crush on a pop star, can have had half the delight I found in the silent admiration I felt for actors and actresses seen 'live' in the bright sunshine.

When I married, in 1929, my husband's grandmother and one of my generous aunts jointly gave us the freehold of number 21 St Leonard's Terrace as a wedding present. For the record it had four bedrooms, a double drawing-room, study, dining-room and all the usual offices as well as little gardens, back and front, and cost £3,500. All of it was on a small scale, but perfect for us. After living there for a few happy years we let it, for economic reasons, and moved to the country. Then came the war. Number 21 was requisitioned, occupied by some Belgians, and fire-bombed. It deteriorated a good deal and sadly we first let it on a long lease and finally sold it. But I have never left Chelsea for very long. After the war we rented for ten years an inconvenient and deafeningly noisy flat in the King's Road, over Mr Kent's toy and sweet shop, opposite Habitat, then the Gaumont Cinema. In 1956 we moved to Elm Park Gardens, where to this day we very much like living.

It is a waste of time to hanker for the past, and I don't. But it was a *good* past, it *did* happen, and I am very grateful to have known Chelsea when King's Road was an overgrown village street of character, with small shops – only Ashby's and Beaton's remain – and not a blue jeans shop, supermarket or men's outfitters to be seen. Number 11 buses actually came on time, and often. Low be it spoken, but I preferred Chelsea when it was on its own and not linked to that other area further north. But, linked or not, it is the Borough that I choose to live in, and St Leonard's Terrace is still one of the prettiest streets not only in London but probably in the entire kingdom.

HESTER MARSDEN-SMEDLEY

Citizen of Chelsea

Joyce Grenfell's death has taken away one of the world's most original and witty entertainers. Chelsea has lost a faithful citizen. She was half American and her interests and work took her to many countries. She had travelled all over the British Isles giving her sparkling performances. But Chelsea was her home and indeed she had lived in or very near Chelsea all her life. Her ageless, lithe figure was well known in the King's Road (where once she lived over a sweet shop). She might be seen watching the evening light on the River Thames. She often wandered in and out of old and new streets, up and down tower blocks. She went shopping in the Fulham Road near which she last lived; in a flat with a view, she delighted to say, looking across trees with changing coloured leaves but always beautiful as trees are, whether covered or bare branches.

Joyce's love of beauty in places, persons, things inspired her powers of observation. She could see beauty where others could not and this all served to make her varied performances so enchanting. She had no training for the theatre except love of life and personal experience. Ordinary people she knew well or had sat next to in a bus or stood behind in queues gave her material. She would adapt often, invent, she said, never. Everything interested her. War years with ENSA, contacts with rich and famous, insight into every walk of life. She was critical where needed, mocking at undue pomp or exaggerated circumstance. But always understanding and kindly.

Much has been written about her plays, films, television, and broadcasting, her books and articles. Here are two little Chelsea stories about her.

36

Once she was compère at a young people's charity ball. There was a remarkably shy youth who was trying to escape from the party. She caught him and to his at first annoyance guided him into a dance. His awkward movements and her grace made an amusing combination. They were soon performing alone in the centre of the floor. He shed his shyness then and there and said much later on he never feared dancing again.

She often played and sang to the old and sick in St Luke's and erstwhile Kingsmead. She bent down beside a bed-ridden patient, then straightened up, smiled and sang a North Country folk song which she alone could interpret from a breathless almost tuneless hum. Then bending down again she gently took the limp hands in hers, patting them together. 'First time I've helped applaud myself,' she said.

JOYCE GRENFELL
A Lovely Wet Day

When I was about eight years old we were seldom given a good long run at doing our own thing. Piano practice, homework from school, meals and being sent out into the nice fresh air interrupted our self-chosen activities. But an all-wet afternoon, with the rain set in for a proper spell, presented us with a blank page of time to be written on in our own way: a bonus space instead of the regular afternoons spent out of doors in all that nice fresh air. In those days I was an indoor girl. I had not yet discovered nature or tennis. On an all-wet afternoon I could do what I most fancied at the time – draw and paint, dress up in my accommodating mother's hats and shoes, and sometimes make fudge, for as long as it took to do these things.

We were London children and lived in a flat without a garden or a balcony. Instead we had the narrow corridor that ran the length of the flat, and that is where we played our active games. By the time I was eight I'd outgrown the corridor, but my brother, aged five, still made motor-bicycle noises with his mouth as he raced his little tricycle up and down, and reversed it at speed (brilliantly) in the doorway of the broom-cupboard. Then he zoomed off again up to the nursery end, and circumnavigated the round table where I was painting. This manœuvre, though skilled, caused the table to jiggle and my paint-water to spill. At such moments these two little birds in their nest did *not* agree . . .

When the unexpected sun came out on what should have been an all-wet afternoon I felt cheated. But my small brother was glad of release into wider spaces, even though at that later hour going out meant nothing more than a short walk on damp pavements, too late to get to the park or our local 'green lung', the Chelsea Pensioners' Gardens. I walked gloomily, wearing my raincoat 'just in case', avoided the pavement joins and wished I was indoors again as my brother progressed in a variety of unorthodox ways, loping along, one foot up and the other in the gutter, or, at a run, played at being a cricketer bowling imaginary balls.

I have grown to like *really* wet walks – that is when I am dressed for the weather in an encompassing plastic raincoat, my old fore-and-aft fisherman's hat, and gummers on my feet. At first I try to stay as dry as I can, but there comes a moment when one is wet enough to abandon the struggle, and a fine sense of recklessness takes over. Then it is good to stride out across fields knee-high in soaking grass, and deliberately choose to splodge through mud at gateways and deep into puddles in the lanes. The getting home again is nice, too; a slight unreasonable feeling of virtue accompanied by relief that it is over, also knowing that, morally, there is no need to go out again that day, rounds off the glow.

What I don't like is trying to keep tidy in best clothes on wet days in towns.

Rain can add light to the city scene – street-lamps reflected, raindrops lit up along railings. Outside my window in London is a beautiful plane tree, an elegant skeleton in winter, an embroidery of tender greens in spring, a thick canopy in summer. I like it most in winter when the heavy left-over seed-pods, like a fat bobble fringe on a Victorian tablecloth, toss in the wet wind, and rain on the bare bones of the tree illumines it with a sleek, wet sea-lion look. Rains come our way from the west, and I see an Impressionist's picture as I lie in bed watching the elegant black branches blurred through my rain-pocked window.

We get plenty of rains in England – or so you might think. Yet when there is a dry spell for longer than three weeks someone is sure to start talking of droughts. I have been in Africa when the rains are supposed to arrive and don't, and I know what it means to scan the vast blue skies looking for rain clouds.

Some clouds pile up, but they are an empty mockery and carry no rain. In the bush you can smell rains coming, and it is a fragrant and moving moment when the skies have blackened and trees lash about in the rising wind, and that unmistakable waft of rain scents the air as it moves in across dry lands. Then all the children run out, arms outstretched, mouths open to catch the drops; and there is rejoicing.

When I was a child I wanted freckles (one wet day I even painted them on my nose). Don't ask me why. I don't know. Walking in the rain I suddenly discovered that rain on the face gave me the feeling I had freckles. And I have never lost this small pleasure. Even now on the rare occasions when I am not trying to keep my hair in curl and have tied it down with a head scarf (or a dainty plastic rain bonnet) I still like lifting up my face and feeling freckled.

JOYCE GRENFELL

Nannies

DRAWINGS BY SIR HUGH CASSON

There now ...

It is fashionable to decry old style nannies and there is reason
for some of the criticism levelled against them. In London, when
I was a child, Hyde Park nannies were very grand indeed. Their
standards of the outward and visible were high; their values
seemed less reliable, but then, they took colour from those who
employed them. There was much competition about the social
position and possessions of their Bosses; over the glossiness of
their prams – some bore coats of arms – and about their charges'
clothes. Some Hyde Park nannies bullied their nursery maids and
sapped the exploratory instincts of the children they looked after
by keeping them close and forbidding games and adventures that
might result in excitement, heat and dirt. Bold spirits were soon
quenched: 'Just look at your hands – and your knees. What will
people think.'

Those of us who moved in less lofty circles, and have known
the comfort and joy of being cared for by the kind of nanny I
had, will join me in singing praises and giving thanks. The kind
of nanny I salute may not have read many books but she was
wise, steady and to be relied on for the unchanging certainty
of selfless love. I now realise my nanny was a socialist as well
as a royalist and nonconformist. She also had a slightly shame-
faced faith in what the tea leaves revealed. Above all she was
good as gold, strong and gentle. She had no formal training but
had learned by doing, first at home, where she helped to look
after the younger children, then at fourteen as a nursery maid

41

under an established nanny. Finally, when she was twenty-one, she left to take on her first baby 'from the month' and turned into a nanny herself. I was her first baby 'from the month' and we loved each other from the day we met until the day she died, fifty-three years later.

All the nannies in my era seem to have conformed to an unwritten law that they should wear grey coats and skirts, white cotton blouses, sensible black shoes, sensible black hats and grey cotton gloves. They wore starched white aprons in the nursery and voluminous flannel ones at bath time. My nanny had a silver brooch called 'MIZPAH' made of clasped hands. She had a white buckram belt that fastened with an interlocking silver buckle and when she bent down to kiss me good night there was the interesting creak of whalebone to be heard.

There were other sounds special to the nursery; the click of a needle pricking through cambric followed by the faint hiss of cotton being drawn tight; the particular plop-plop nanny made as she tested the temperature of my bath water with her elbow and said: 'There now.' She said 'There now' a good deal. After she had buttoned my blunt-toed shoes she patted the soles,

removed me from her lap and said, 'There now, down you get.'

Unlike most mothers today nannies only led one life at a time and that life was fully dedicated to the nursery where a familiar repeat-pattern of days, as well as responses, made the climate a good one to grow roots in. One gained confidence enough to take on wider adventuring when the time came for it and in my case, I was encouraged to be independent. There was no maternal 'smother-love' loving in our kind of nursery; common sense and kindness prevailed. Successful nannies were not over-protective, for they knew the world could be a rough place and their job was to equip us so we could get along in it. They also knew that encouragement helps.

'Not bad, all things considered.'

'Now you can do better next time.'

'It's silly to say you can't – of course you can – you'll manage.'

So you did a bit better, and managed. One marvels now at

the patience and enduring good temper of nannies bombarded by repeated 'why's.' The answers were not always satisfying:

'Because I say so.'

'Don't ask silly questions, dear.'

'But, Nanny...?'

'But me no buts.'

Little bits of nanny-wisdom have stayed with me for ever. I still 'undo' my coat when I go into a warm atmosphere so that I may 'feel the benefit later'. At tea I still 'start plain and finish sweet' and when I am tempted to eat in a rush I can still hear that quiet voice saying – 'Don't bolt, ducky, eat sensibly.'

In her book *A Late Beginner* Priscilla Napier has a good ear for nanny murmurings. She lived in Egypt until she was eight. She and her nanny had been to look at the Pyramids.

'What are they for, Nanny?'

'Tombs, dear... Where's your other sock?'

'Who put them there?'

'The Pharaohs did ...'

'Waiting for the Last Trump?'

'Yes,' Nanny said knowing better than to hesitate. 'Your other sock is in the doll's bed and that it got there by itself I beg to doubt.'

Priscilla Napier also pinpoints nanny's insularity:

'Cress!' Nanny said, 'In *France*. The very idea!' and, later, 'You should know better than to lose your temper in front of foreigners.'

Another nanny in another context was taken to see the great windows in Chartres Cathedral. 'It's a very dim light to sew by,' she said.

Nanny-talk invokes for me the firmness of a loving hand with a hair brush, a face flannel and buttons. 'There now.' remember red coal fires and the pleasant smell of vests airing on the nursery fire guard; the click of a clock and the blessed ordinariness of that small, safe world in which we were given the time and the quiet to develop and grow sturdy. I am grateful to be reminded of a good and happy time.

FRANCES GRENFELL

My Sister-in-Law

Joyce was my first in-law, the first outsider to penetrate our close family circle and widen its circumference. To a pair of small sisters at the tail end of that family it was quite an experience, for it had never occurred to them that any of their elder brothers or sisters would marry. That was something only grown-ups did; from their view, at the ages of nine and eleven, it was a happening as remote as dying.

It must have been daunting for Joyce to be faced with this new family. In-laws usually require a bit of absorbing, and these were numerous and varied. My mother (Reggie's stepmother, Hilda) needs a dozen pens to describe her, as in all her diverse interests and actions she not only aroused in her family great love, but often total exasperation. Besides this exceptionally surprising character, who bicycled in trousers, but with her dress pinned up with safety-pins ready to be lowered when she took her trousers off after reaching her destination; who in her eighties spent many happy hours translating Teilhard de Chardin, and who never relented from trying to make her family do things which at that moment they particularly did not want to do, Joyce acquired a father-in-law, a brother-in-law, and no fewer than five sisters-in-law.

One thing my mother never excelled at – or tried to excel at – was handing on to her daughters any clothes sense, or even advice on the sheer practicalities of life. The clothes for the youngest members of the family were either bought in frantic Saturday-morning shopping sessions in Harvey Nichols, where two of everything were chosen, or concocted from yards of unlikely and strange material sent to any old dressmaker,

45

probably picked because she was a starving refugee. It all ended in one fat and one thin little girl being poured into the same outfit, both feeling self-conscious and furious.

Joyce was immediately recognised wholeheartedly, and no doubt with relief by her mother-in-law, as someone who not only knew about Those Things, but was interested in them. 'Dressing alike' came to an end. Quite often Joyce took on the shopping expeditions, or chose the material and the dressmaker. Buying clothes became an exciting pleasure.

Joyce was now an authority to appeal to. She always respected the imagination of children and treated them with that rare gift which made them feel grown-up and contemporaries. So fascination, surprise, and a fresh world of romance and gaiety were our first impressions of our new sister-in-law.

Joyce became for ever the family's expert and arbitrator in all matters sartorial. When she was young she was fashionable; unlike her in-laws she did not leave her clothes to chance. She rarely wore anything severe, and I can never remember her in black; something always flowed, and there was softness and colour. The dresses she designed for her own wedding were glamorous and romantic; the bridesmaids in white velvet with long medieval sleeves lined with green velvet.

At family weddings Joyce was usually dressing the bride, adjusting a veil or a wreath, and even occasionally dispatching a recalcitrant bridesmaid to have her hair seen to. Her confederate on these occasions was Minnie, our nanny, who admired and approved Joyce's expertise and orderliness in organising this side of the proceedings. It was not surprising that Joyce figured so much at family weddings, as she was a romantic in its best sense: in her love of beauty and harmony and her expectation of happy endings.

It also fell to Joyce to help and advise the sisters-in-law in a lot of practical details. She was acutely aware of the agonies teenagers go through, when embarrassments can become crises. It was she who gave me Odo-ro-no and face powder, and I even remember an early lipstick called Tangee, which I was sure for a long time was the last word in sophistication. Once when sitting nervously in a train thinking of the possible pitfalls facing me at the week-end party I was *en route* for, I heard the sound of running feet coming down the platform. It was my mother, who pressed a small parcel into my hand saying breathlessly: 'Joyce gave it me. Use very very little, and never tell your father.' It was a small tin of rouge.

Even at this time Joyce tried to teach us basic common sense in dressing: 'Choose one colour as a foundation and then you can cut down on bags and hats and shoes.' When her youngest sister-in-law Laura was going to New Zealand as the Governor-General's wife, Joyce immediately took charge of her wardrobe. Laura had never spent much time or money on her clothes. Once during the war, when she had moved into W.V.S. uniform and a much-loved pair of sheepskin-lined boots for the duration, her brother, on leave, rebelled when she walked into a London restaurant for dinner in her 'woolly' boots. But now she tried hard to learn from Joyce; she knew she must do her best. Joyce gave her a Victor Stiebel evening gown, and although the fitting sessions filled her with terror it boosted her morale like nothing else. One day she went to luncheon with a friend to show off some of the wondrous new clothes, saying: 'I just want you to see – I've really got the hang of it. At last I'm smart.' The friend sighed. The clothers were lovely, but the hat, gloves and shoes were in three different colours.

Joyce threw herself with enthusiasm into any project which involved decorating a house. She and her mother-in-law had merging tastes. Their sense of colour and light was very similar; both liked a measure of simplicity. Not for them elaborate flower arrangements; flounces were controlled, rooms lit by lamps not ceiling lights. They always took genuine pleasure in each other's homes and frequently enjoyed and used each other's ideas. The flower table in Joyce's flat originated in a family home.

When Joyce arrived, almost imperceptibly the songs sung

round the piano changed from 'The Lass of Richmond Hill' and 'Early One Morning' to the latest current popular successes. With these came the stories and the mimics and the characters. Sitting round the drawing-room fire in the evening, in the family home in Wales in pre-television days, urged on by the children, Joyce would start a character. Shirl and her boy-friend Norm came early, in a lot of different guises, and there was the nervous débutante making inane conversation, and an older character who used Joyce's special 'mouth', with the tongue folded over the bottom teeth. Often the events that had actually happened during the day were relived through the eyes of these imaginary people. In a way when she first made them public, a tiny bit of that family audience almost resented them being so exposed, they were such a real world to young imaginations.

It wasn't at first all that easy for Laura and me to assimilate her public acclaim and famous image. For us she was a steady, loving, funny, available sister.

Laura was killed by a falling tree in a storm a fortnight after Joyce died. Their lives had led them into very different fields, but a closeness remained, and it was strangely natural and comforting to think of them journeying on together.

JOYCE GRENFELL

Small Fry

This is going to be a fan article, written from a distance, about children. From a distance, because I write as a selfish, childless looker-on who gets immense pleasure from other people's children.

I like and enjoy children. Not *all* children any more than all grown-ups, music, books or hats. But for the most part I find them fascinating and attractive, from the first pinky-mauve days to when their teeth start dropping out and they turn into schoolchildren; and from then on, too, through the ten-to-twelve doldrums to when they become Young People; and even then.

From a looking-on point of view I suppose they are best at about eighteen months; or at two. No, maybe they are best at three; or possibly four – it is impossible to say.

I particularly like originals of about three. There is an American friend with a grandchild I have never seen, but the stories of Holly's goings-on and the pictures of Holly's wild beauty have aroused my interest and I am her fan.

When she was three she got up from her bed one summer evening and walked slowly through the living-room without a stitch on. A rather surprised young man, a stranger, was sitting in there waiting for the family to meet before supper. Holly glided by him in silence, and then, as she was about to leave by another door, said, as if in explanation: 'I've been having a temperature.'

Holly told someone who had asked her if she liked to play with dolls: 'No, I play with cobwebs best.'

Watching children, particularly when they don't know you are doing so, is a particular pleasure. Those quick changes of mood, for instance. Small boys who dribble an imaginary football down the street and then get more interested in trying to balance on the edge of the kerb. And then stand quite still to think for a few seconds before jumping up and down with their feet together for no special reason, except that they feel like jumping up and down. Maybe the fact that I no longer feel in the least like jumping up and down adds to the interest.

I once watched a child of about two-and-a-half trying to stamp on little waves breaking across a wide Cornish beach. She stretched her hands out in pleasure with every little stamp and her bathing pants fell lower and lower, till she jumped them off altogether but didn't notice it, so intent was she on the important job of stamping on those waves. She sang to herself a sort of monotone running commentary on what she was doing and the sound of it, mingled with soft sea noises, made a most pleasing music.

Some time ago my housekeeper had to go away for a while, and her place was taken by an Austrian friend with a five-year-old daughter. Liesl couldn't be left at home, so she came to work too. She was very fair, nicely rounded, with fierce blue eyes and more curiosity than any human being I have ever met. In her it was an energy that if harnessed could have run an entire electrical plant. There was nothing idle about it, she wanted to *know*, and nothing short of picking her up bodily and removing her from the room could stop her knowing.

Her voice was a most attractive mixture of her mother's Austrian and her father's Welsh.

[*Joyce wrote a poem about this child, calling her 'Miss Belt'*]

Miss Belt is four.
Her mother is a Viennese,
Her father is from Wales.

Miss Belt is fair,
Square,
With honey hair tied with two red bows
Into two paint-brushes,
So tightly tied
Her eyebrows rise in surprise.

She stands and stares and concentrates.

Sometimes she concentrates on me:
   'Are you goin' out?
   Are you hungry?
   Is det your *best* skairt?
   Are you vairy old?
   Sell aie tell you a STORY?'

The answer is NO to all these questions but the last.

   'Vuncerponcertime...
   Sell aie tell you Hansel and Gretel?
   Or Schinderallar?
   Or Schnow-Vhite?
   Or Pater Pahn?
   Or Hansel and Gretel?'

So it is Hansel and Gretel.

   'Vell, Hansel and Gretel vas livin' in die vood
   All die time.
   Is it tea time?'

Not yet.

   'Hansel and Gretel vas livin' in die vood
   All day and *all* night.'

She concentrates on an interesting scratch
Upon her knee,
Then stares as at a vision into space
Her eyes enormous,
Rapture on her face.

'Is it yet time for *tea*?'

No, not yet.

'Oh.
Hansel and Gretel vasn't *gairls*
Dey vas *vun* gairl and *vun* boy!'

I see.

'Is it now time for tea?'

Annabel is a favourite friend of mine. She was three when we first met. She was daisy picking, one at a time, and then bringing each decapitated flower for inspection. She grunted down into picking position and then said to the world at large: 'When I are asleep I don't know nothing of me.'

Annabel doesn't favour war. She thinks it is bad.

I have a middle-aged cousin who lived as a child in Virginia. She made family history over an incident concerning a lie. She said she had seen a lion in the rose garden. She was sent upstairs to stand in a dark corner to reflect and ask God's pardon. When she was sorry she could come down. I will call her Emily Parker. At last she left the dark corner and reported to her mother.

'Did you ask God to forgive you, Emily?'

'Yes, I did.'

'What did He say?'

'He said, "That's funny, Miss Parker, because for a minute I thought it was a lion, too."'

I must confess that I am not absolutely mad about children in trains. This is partly because I am apt to use trains for small slices of quiet between rushes, and I count on the time spent in them for recuperative purposes; and partly just selfishness.

I once wrote a terrible poem that began: 'I love little children, but NOT in the train.' This was after a journey in the company of a character called Eric, who was about three and who had a lot of surplus energy that he used by hitting the door with the window strap. He did this for a very long time. It was very loud. Our journey was a very long one ...

Watching children watching a conjuror or listening to a story is a great delight; so is watching children dancing or doing gym. In fact watching children is wonderful.

I am sentimental about babies, particularly babies who smell like new buns and who coo and laugh and bite their toes and are civil to me when I speak to them. I like that intoxicating moment when a baby isn't sure whether it is going to cry and the lower lip turns down and the eyes look surprised and then suddenly it decides to abandon the whole thing and yawns. Then follows what I take to be a sigh of contentment. It may of course be wind. In any case it is probably relief. You see I'm ignorant. I don't know. I just enjoy children.

VIRGINIA GRAHAM

Best Friend

Although I knew Joyce when I was five, we did not become staunch and everlasting friends until we were in our early teens, when we found each other so irresistibly funny, so wildly entertaining, we formed a sort of mutual admiration society that continued, I am proud to say, until she died. We also shared an unorthodox religion, Christian Science, which, in those unecumenical days, entailed a certain amount of gentle persecution; and as we ate our baked beans on toast at Lyons Corner House before going to a matinée – and we did this nearly every week, though sometimes, to be dashing, we changed to Welsh rarebit – we would air our doubts and convictions, nodding wisely, like very old owls, as we pondered on the Creation, or later in the meal, between sucks at our Strawberry Nut Sundaes, on eternity.

Of course, all public conversations with Joyce, even at this early stage, were prone to interruption, for if the people next door were in any way interesting she would tell me to shut up as she wanted to listen. Many of my views on immortality, or indeed on the theatre or the price of eggs, were faded out by Joyce's incurable habit of eavesdropping.

All through her life she overheard amusing or amazing remarks on buses or trains, at concerts or on street corners, and sometimes I would accuse her of inventing them; but I don't think she did. Her awareness of what was going on around her was acute and constant, and this not only formed the basis of her future career but gave her the aura of joyful expectancy that was so attractive.

It was quite impossible to be depressed in Joyce's company,

for wherever she was, in whatever circumstance, she was ready
and waiting to be blessed by some potential joy. I have never
known anyone look forward so much; she was always running
(metaphorically speaking, for she was not much of a runner
otherwise) to meet the sight, the song, the scent, the joke. I do
not believe she was bored by a single minute of her life, for every
country walk had a sedge warbler or a wood anemone round
the corner, every T.V. programme, however dire, contained
some small commendable thing. And there was music waiting
everywhere. Yet though her capacity for enjoyment was limitless, she cleverly managed not to be a Pollyanna. She avoided
saying a downpour was nice for the ducks in favour of a story
about a duck. Or, perhaps, a downpour. One never felt that
she was pi, though in point of fact she had very high standards.
Possibly in her youth the strong puritanical streak in her was
more pronounced than it later became, when the stern outline
between black and white grew smudged with forgiveness, or at
any rate, understanding. All the same you wanted Joyce to think
well of you, largely because she would be so disappointed that
her swan had an element of goose in it. She really doted on goodness.

As a friend her main virtue – and she had many subsidiary
ones – was her reliability. She was not mercurial: whatever the
temperature she did not change. She was as steady, and come
hell or high water, as comforting as a nanny, and like that
moribund figure there was not an ounce of malice in her. There
were times, certainly in her professional life, when she was badly
treated, but she seemed incapable of being angry or bearing ill-
will. She could admonish, and indeed frequently did so; the
queue jumper and the theatre chatterer getting their ears gently
knocked back, much to their surprise; but it was in a reformatory
rather than an exasperated style.

This nanny side of Joyce (or what she called her Bossy-boots
side) is one that her public, naturally enough, knew little about.
My husband, having carried the deadweight of her handbag a
few yards, once asked her to empty its contents on to a table,

and from its recesses there appeared every device, contrivance, aid and solace known to man: sewing equipment, washing materials, maps, pens, collapsible cutlery, drawing-pins, Kleenex, scent, cosmetics, sticking plaster, and a radio. I remember once asking Joyce, rather sarcastically, whether she happened to have a piece of beige braid about her person, and she said, 'Well yes, as a matter of fact I *have*!' One felt very safe with Joyce.

Oddly enough, the only thing that fussed her was time. Although fundamentally confident that 'time is no part of eternity', she took a pessimistic view of the day's speed, and was incorrigibly unpunctual, arriving at least an hour too early for every appointment. She liked to get where she was going as soon as possible and stay there, either sitting in the car listening to the radio, or walking around assimilating local colour 'until ready', so to speak. I am much the same way, so that I have shared with her, along with our patient husbands, many a waiting hour sitting in empty theatres, or in concert halls with only the drummer tuning his drums as company, strolling round towns, or catching the train before. The trouble about this time fixation is that you only need to be a minute late for your friends to start ringing the hospitals.

Friendship, to my mind, defies all attempts at analysis. Byron said it was 'Love without his wings', Goldsmith that it was 'a disinterested commerce between equals', but it remains for me indefinable. A harbour, certainly; and yet deeper than that. Joyce and I had many different tastes, and by right these should have clashed. She genuinely preferred the daisy to the lily, comfort to elegance, the bacon sandwich in the cafeteria to caviar at the Ritz. She liked to holiday quietly in wide open spaces, whereas I like sightseeing; she was gregarious and I am not, and there were many other ways in which our paths diverged. Nevertheless our friendship never flickered for an instant from the true. That we both loved the same kind of music and books and plays was a great bond, and that we had the same sense of humour an even greater one. We also shared many friends, although admittedly she had hundreds I never met and who were just recurring names with easily confused histories.

An irrepressible correspondent, her pen-pals were spread in layers across the globe, and to each she gave her interest and attention. Her letters to me are full of the minutiae of daily living, for she was a great lover of detail. Concurrent with her views on the contemporary scene, or on the plight of friends, or on something fascinating she had read or heard, there would be news of how she and Reggie had gone into Cockermouth at 10.10 a.m. and bought a reel of cotton, some peppermints, another toothbrush and two apples; or of how her hotel bedroom in Leeds was furnished; or what they had had for luncheon in a restaurant in Sydney. These letters, written daily when she was not in London, provide a thorough survey of the world's development over the past fifty years in all fields save the political (in which she was only marginally interested), and as fodder for future historians they are surely invaluable. Literary masterpieces no, for Joyce wrote at great speed and just as she spoke (she also wrote to a *great* many people); but if anybody wants to know the price of a Melton Mowbray pie in 1962 or what one wore to go to a wedding in 1949, it is all here. Here too, in detail, a world assortment of people and birds and flowers, all of which she loved. Incidentally, in writing letters she not only demanded of herself full particulars, but also accuracy, once going so far as to put an asterisk against the word Dreft and a footnote reading, 'It wasn't Dreft I bought, it was Flash!'

Although I am steeped in comforting metaphysics I miss Joyce very much. Every morning, when we were in England, she rang me at 8.20 sharp, and even if, latterly, we did not see each other a great deal, as she was concerned with the promotion of her books, we knew each other's itineraries down to the last particular, and, as Bacon wrote, our friendship doubled joys and 'cutteth griefs in halves'.

I sit here, thinking about my old friend sadly and yet with enormous pleasure. I can see her and hear her very distinctly:

reading out the clues of *The Times* crossword, not always correctly, after luncheon on Saturday; singing in the kitchen as she brewed her famous soups; picking tiny bunches of wild flowers and marvelling at them; talking about God; waltzing with Reggie; tying the knot in my scarf the *right* way so that it lay flat; and telling me I had spinach between my teeth. And of course I miss *her* teeth; and her fringe, whose state of curliness was a constant source of anxiety; and her small busy hands writing or sewing or painting; and all those funny caps and brightly coloured shirts and the dozens of uncomfortable shoes.

But above all the laughter. I spent my childhood laughing with my father and the rest of my life laughing with Joyce. So I cannot complain. And I do not. But understandably things seem very quiet at the moment.

JOYCE GRENFELL

Father and Daughter

[*In her autobiographies Joyce took care not to dwell on the break-up of her parents' marriage and the unhappiness it caused, but this is poignantly evoked in this poem written in 1953.*]

Oh, the sadness of the evening after tea!
The window-panes are pocked with tears
That blur the shrill viridian lawns;
The robin spills his little silver beads of song
And tears my heart in me.

Within the room my father sits
Existing in his chair
While Hindemith
(Bassoon and piano)
Unrejoicing on the Third
Bickers through the evening air.

The lead in the old man's feet and hanging hands
Weighs in my heart and in my head.
Where is that laughing creature, mountain high,
The dear companion of another day?

We walked together then, on Saturdays
Went to the galleries and heard the Proms,
Saw the play from the pit,
And argued and walked and talked and walked and walked,
Father and daughter,
Liking the same poor puns,
Meeting on common ground.

His judgments all were true,
I had no doubts at all,
He knew.

Where is he now, the tall young man who was my father?
Moving clumsily in our nursery games;
Then tennis, rounders on the beach,
Telling us the short prosaic stories that we loved
Of men in bowlers called Mr Blenkinsop
Or Mr Peppercorn or Mr Bilk.

Who is this I see instead
Existing in his small stiff chair?
The world shrinks to the size of an empty nut.
Where is he now, oh where?

STEPHEN POTTER

The Grenfell Experience

[Stephen Potter wrote this in 1953. He died in 1969.]

It was quite a good idea to let Joyce Phipps go to the Royal Academy of Dramatic Art. She certainly had the looks for an actress; she certainly worked reasonably hard in a rather abstract way, abstract because nobody really believed that the stage was going to be her career. She would be married almost instantly, that was certain. Then would come social life plus even a job, but not theatre, everybody knew that. Joyce was as straightforward as her name, with none of the trace of mania or crankiness which rightly or wrongly people nearly always associate with acting.

Nevertheless, the R.A.D.A. will do as a finishing school, even if the student doesn't make much headway with Molière; even if she finds comic, if only slightly so, that elaborate drill of getting up, sitting down, and walking into a room by numbers which is known to all drama students as Basic Movement.

Well, she did marry, almost sooner than instantly, and very delightfully. In fact, this story begins, you will see, like a nice lending-library novel; with Mrs Grenfell (as she had become) turning out to be gifted with artisitic and literary talents, and all set for heroine.

I got to know her about the time the story took an unconventional or at any rate an unexpected turning. I knew the name Joyce Grenfell because she had recently become (for the *Observer*) one of the two or three radio critics who took their work extremely seriously, and who treated this difficult and tenuous art, which was then my art, with respect. At last Potters met Grenfells at the house of friends. Joyce had heard that morning in the country a woman speaking at a Village Institute, one of those nice bright people whose advice is so helpful, but yet whose cheerfulness casts a chill. Joyce described the woman, and then suddenly and naturally *became* the woman. That was the shock. I stared at Joyce. She was talking about acceptable gifts, an easy way to make jolly posies. 'When you are making husk flowers,' she was saying, 'do not confine yourselves to *boutonnières*. Be bold about it. You can always make great sprays of delphs or lupes.'

Was ever a challenge so masterful made from lips so suffocated by refinement? I don't think we laughed so very much then, and I think it was because, for the first time, we were undergoing the 'Grenfell experience'. By this, I mean that Joyce's reflection of the character was so exact that it seemed to be the character herself who was speaking. I felt as if the observation was being made by myself.

'Marvellous,' we all thought: but one's friends so often were marvellous. Was it just a trick? I wasn't sure, but I did want an opinion from some of my friends. So the Potters specially asked the Grenfells when the Francis Meynells and the Laurence Gilliams, of the B.B.C., were coming, about as much as our house would hold. And we had particularly asked Herbert and Joan Farjeon. After dinner, I said to Joyce, 'Tell us about that woman at the Village Institute.' She had not done it since as any sort of 'turn'. Nothing was written down. But it seemed somehow better. No mistake about the laughter, this time. I remember especially watching Bertie Farjeon's face, as he sat on the floor. Then Bertie asked her on the spot to come into his new revue, *The Little Revue*, and star in it as her first professional engagement.

It was an exciting first night. There is all the difference in the world between the amateur in the drawing-room and the amateur in the cast of professionals.

Everybody was right. She was a success, and she was still an amateur. She still looks rather awkward, and out of place, making her entrance in the finale of a revue. 'It's those wonderful *gestures*,' said Alastair Sim of her, when Joyce was the gym mistress in his film. But they are always gestures from her note-book, never from stock and, when she is with professionals, this is not always an advantage.

Soon after Joyce Grenfell was settling down to her new job of the theatre, I was settling down to my new job of writing and producing for the B.B.C. In between wartime regimental programmes I was asked for a new programme to provide war-time light relief. A series called 'How' was the result. It began stumblingly – 'How to make a speech', 'How to argue'. Then I thought of Joyce.

Good broadcasting needs two things: lightness of touch and distinctness of personality. I thought that even in the presence of that stony-hearted old microphone Joyce Grenfell would be able to achieve this. She did.

In an eight-year collaboration, she learned something about broadcasting from me but I learned five times as much from her. The essential in radio writing is to give pictures, to write for the eye. As Joyce spoke, we saw. For instance, one of the many characters she created for our programmes was a rather difficult little boy called Sidney. Sidney is never seen, of course; he never even speaks. But the way his form mistress talks encouragingly to him, making the best of him so worriedly, makes Sidney, to me, shine forth like fire. Does Sidney, we ask her, listen to the radio?

J.G.: Come along, Sidney; do you ever listen to the wireless? No, dear, don't do that. Pay attention, dear. The gentleman's asking you if you ever listen to the wireless. You do, don't you, Sidney? You like Toy Town, don't you, Sidney? You see, he is smiling. I think that evokes quite a memory. And music we have in the morning. You like that, don't you Sidney? He's not very musical, as a matter of fact.

Oh, the pain of his teacher's smile, wider and wider as Sidney looks blacker and blacker.

Production days with Joyce Grenfell and with our favourite cast were pure pleasure. Has she no faults? Her appeal is wide –

Home, Light and Third; but nobody can like a girl on every wavelength. Personally, I am less fond of her Light: some of the songs and characters like Shirley's Girl Friend seem more nearly typed, more conventional. But never elsewhere does she lose her freshness.

Lunch with Joyce (she is always exactly punctual, another slight fault) means beginning with a tiny portrait gallery of the people she has seen and heard on the bus and in the greengrocer's, who make brief appearances round the menu when we are ordering food. It is a good start, because always Joyce seems to like her characters, and her characters like her. It is as if her Mrs Mopp, her charwoman character, for instance, was the Mrs Mopp part of Joyce Grenfell.

Perhaps that is why her satire never hurts. Boswell criticised Johnson's celebrated comment on the death of Garrick, 'that it eclipsed the gaiety of nations and diminished the public stock of harmless pleasure'. Put that way round it is an anticlimax, Boswell thought. He was wrong. Genius especially and genius alone can make the harmlessness of an art its most positive and vital quality.

'But what is she like as a friend, what is she like to talk to?' (Always a difficult question, with someone you know well.)

'Well, for instance, is she musical?' Oh yes, very much so. Music is a big part of her life. Bach is her first, by a long way, but like most musicians, she would not divide her music into 'classical' and 'light', whatever that means. She was, incidentally, one of the very first to have the recordings of *Guys and Dolls* sent over.

If you were to ask me whether she is fond of flowers I should say that she doesn't really know much about them, loves to be given them, likes to use them in her careful room decoration with, this year, rather graceful bits of trailing ivy, twisted around. Ivy is the green-hungry Londoner's salve. Joyce Grenfell has brief spurts of wanting to go to the country, but quickly and happily comes trooping back to the dust and traffic of King's Road.

Compared to my own, her life seems more crisp and well-ordered. When we are working together, she keeps me to the point of what we are writing. She gets through more telephoning and writing without a secretary than I do with one. If I am about to see her, I find myself saying, 'Now wake up, don't be floppy or sloppy or you may miss something.' And I must not, with her, out of laziness or vagueness, say what I don't mean. 'You're not *listening*,' she will say. Or she will extract my little bit of insincerity on a pin, as it were, and show it to me.

Something else equally obvious is that she is what is called a 'good' person, if one can allow so boring a word to be used of such an unboring person. If things are going wrong, or if somebody is ill, or if there's a really tough bit of entertaining to do in a good cause, Joyce will be there without the faintest suggestion that she is conferring a favour by doing all she can.

BETTY HARDY

Joyce and Stephen

Joyce made her first 'big solo' broadcast in October 1941, in seven of her sketches produced by Stephen Potter. She had only a couple of hours' rehearsal before performing them live – a demanding job, which she did so successfully that the staff in the control room were reduced to helpless laughter.

Soon after that she came as a guest artist in a series called 'Weekly Radiogram', which was organised by an old friend of hers, Leslie Perowne, and consisted of interviews alternating with records of popular music to give members of the Forces a chance to send messages to their families.

I had seen Joyce in *Diversion*, but had not met her, so that I was not prepared for the surprising way in which she established warm welcoming contact, and set everyone at ease. On this occasion there were two lads, one an able seaman of the Royal Navy, and the other an American enlisted man.

Joyce drew them both out to talk about themselves.

'Where do you come from?' she asked the American.

'North Carolina, ma'am.'

'Why,' said Joyce, 'I come from Virginia. That makes us practically kin.' I can hear her voice now – 'That makes us practically kin.'

The boy blushed with pleasure as she repeated it; and the broadcast became a family party of welcome.

Afterwards I went back to the B.B.C. repertory company in Manchester, which was headed by that wonderful radio artist, Gladys Young, with Ronald Simpson, Carleton Hobbs, Norman Shelley, Geoffrey Wincott and others. Sometimes we did as many as six broadcasts a week, with a great variety of subjects. Plays, documentary features about the war and war conditions, adaptations of classic novels, poetry readings. All were done live, which gave them an immediacy of contact with all the listeners in their homes waiting for the siren.

Laurence Gilliam had gathered round him a team of experts in directing as well as writing the broadcast material. Stephen Potter was in charge of most of the literary features, and wrote many himself, scripts which would stand comparison with some of the best of the present time. He had a gift of conveying whole passages of life, and a whole involved character, in a few sentences. He once gave me Mrs Samuel Taylor Coleridge, that distressed 'Minnow among Tritons', and the enclosing and alarming drama of her life, with a sharp economy of words.

The 'How' series, started as a demonstration of how to achieve success in various crafts and activities, was founded on Stephen's own personal achievements. He was a man of great intensity of feeling, a musician with perfect pitch, acute in all his observations. As an all-round athlete he was a cruel and far-ranging croquet player. I watched him in a game with Maurice Thierry, a visiting radio commentator from France, who had a powerful grasp mentally, but a large and solid frame. He lamented when Stephen whacked the balls far away at every combat, leaving his fat friend in an impossible position, as with crows of pride he won the game. Stephen was a winner in most things, but I think his greatest inspiration was to open the way to Joyce's career, presenting her to Herbert Farjeon, who immediately recognised the quality of her gift and straightway put her into his revue.

Joyce was already established and in great demand when Stephen asked her to collaborate with him in writing and performing in a new 'How' series – involving a greater use of satire, and more sheer entertainment.

In Joyce he had the perfect partner. Her wit and invention, and her supreme power of observation, as well as her sure knowledge of what makes an audience laugh, became an inexhaustible power to him. He collected those of us who usually worked with him in radio, and we all were excited at the prospect, but those new scripts were a revelation. When we started to read them it was not with the usual swift appraisal of lines at a first reading, it was with astonishment and delight at the brilliance and sharpness of the humour. Joyce gave us many surprises in the voices she invented or created from some voice she had heard and noted. The first time we heard Fern Brixton the rehearsal collapsed into gasping laughter. The work for all of us was lit up by her spirit. I remember that there were never any difficulties. She had a way of being above it, above all anxiety or worry, a quality she shared with Sir Tyrone Guthrie who used to call out at any crucial moment in production, 'Rise above it! Rise above it!'

Joyce had that high serenity which makes me think of a lark, singing so clearly up in the sky.

J. C. TREWIN

Voices at the Party

Joyce Grenfell recalled that, when she and Nellie Wallace were working at a country cinema in a wartime concert, she heard Nellie mutter: 'What *does* she think she's doing out there on her own, talking to herself?' This was another way of saying what Gertrude does when Hamlet addresses the Ghost in the Closet Scene: 'Alas, how is't with you, That you do bend your eye on vacancy, And with th'incorporal air do hold discourse?'

Clearly, Nellie Wallace was not an audience for the monologue; to describe how this 'talking to herself' sounded might have baffled her. There, at least, she would have joined a good many drama critics. As Ivor Brown wrote (and he would repeat it to me often), they have usually been shy of dissecting a voice. Few people, after all, hear precisely the same thing; what seems to one of them a reasonable analogy can appear eccentric to another. Much stage history is a web of impressions; of Irving's voice as 'muffled-bright, forking like lightning through mist'; or the young Forbes-Robertson's in Shaw's resolute comparison to 'the chalumeau register of a clarionet'. The writer can only try: too often, as in O'Casey's phrase about a telephone, a knot or a twist or a tangle 'keeps the sound from travellin''. Approximations multiply; but what was the voice really like? Sedulously, scholars will comb the prompt-book of a classical production; yet no stage-manager's detail can tell us just how a player sounded. Hamlet's word is 'We'll *hear* a play'. We cannot hear it from a prompt-book.

So much is now recorded and preserved that later historians should be luckier. But will they be lucky? It is one thing to have the voice, another to fix it in print. Remembering Joyce

Grenfell, we sympathise with the chameleon defeated by a tartan scarf.

The Grenfell voices, dozens of them, were in the theatre through nearly forty years. It all began in John Street, Adelphi, down behind the Strand and even then shadowed by a hideous office block. No trace remains now of the Little Theatre, soberly compact, host to *Dracula* and Chekhov, Grand Guignol and Shaw. Herbert Farjeon's revues, controlled by the wittiest theatre mind of his period, came late. In April 1939, after a burlesque of *Magyar Melody* (Romany Roma and Romany Roy) had been blacked out during the first half of *The Little Revue*, lights rose on a visiting lecturer (grey chiffon and red jacket; tall and embracingly genial). Addressing us as 'Madam President, Fellow Institute Members', and raking the house with an inclusive beam, she urged us in tones comradely, coy, and frequently in italics, to make Useful and Acceptable Gifts, '*so* easy to dispose of'. A boutonnière, perhaps, said the voice, flaring confidently on the last syllable. Why not a boutonnière from *empty* beech-nut husk clusters? 'Cleanse your husks thoroughly.' The speaker, pushing forward, head slightly on one side, peered round the Institute to ensure we had understood her. And why – every syllable glittering – should we confine ourselves to boutonnières? 'Be *bold* about it! You can make great sprays of lupes, or delphs.'

The summons was a clarion. So we could. We were ready for most things, even wastepaper-basket tins ('Cleanse your tin *thoroughly*'), or 'Dicky Calendars' from 'two india-rubbers, or, as we called them, when I went to school, *bunjies*' – the first unveiling of a tone familiar one day in the Grenfell kindergarten. We had heard nothing quite like this. Far off, at the beginning of the century, there had been the nearly mythical Cissie Loftus. Florence Desmond and Elizabeth Pollock were variously applauded mimics between the wars. But then Joyce Grenfell's was not (and never would be) direct mimicry of A or Y or Z from the front page. It was the recreation of a type, the work of a new artist in the monologue. Ruth Draper, yes; but she was Olympian

and alone, never to be an incident in a West End revue. A
monologue in revue had been an exercise, formidably, trans-
iently theatrical, a diversion that in a few hours would have
slipped out of mind like a snow-wreath in thaw. Now here
was someone who before this had entertained only for the fun
of the thing; she would be – though it would have surprised her
to know it – an enduring voice of the English theatre.

Two years after her début (the 'Mothers' triptych as well –
'Do you think you could be really happy married to a middle-
aged Portuguese conjuror?') the Little Theatre – nightly at nine –
had been bombed into ruin. Long afterwards a librettist on
another stage would look back at it: 'Brightness tonight falls
from the air./Only our memories can repair/A blazing theatre,
and renew/The ashes of that last revue.' For Joyce Grenfell and
her gathered voices it had been the beginning of a career that
would take her across the world, and, in the parish of the
London theatre, to Wyndham's and the Piccadilly, the St
Martin's and the Fortune, the Lyric (Hammersmith), the
Queen's, and the Theatre Royal, Haymarket. Once we had
heard her at the Little, we seemed to find her again daily. Half-
eavesdropping in a restaurant, a foyer, in tube or bus, at a meeting or party, we caught fragments of speech that could only be
hers, a vowel genteelly high-lighted or simply splintered, an
effusive greeting, a few words suddenly over-pitched, a mild
enormity, a platitude enunciated (in the way of platitudes) with
dazzling clarity. Joyce Grenfell heard more intensely than most
people; when she heard she analysed; from what she analysed
she selected with a connoisseur's pleasure in fine shades, the
accents of privet-clipped suburbia, the Brixton Road, the
Chiltern village. It was not mimicry in the roughest sense that
for a moment she could sound like someone in the news easily
recognisable, and pass to another and another, using the more
obvious mannerisms. That was the method of the 'protean
artist', a creditable performance of himself in half-a-dozen
attitudes (and wigs) and against the clock, believing fervently
that every moment his personality changed. Joyce Grenfell

seldom approximated, though now and then in her early days she could broaden unwarily. But the voice soon became more like an accurate, animated recording of her subject than (Ivor Brown again) a player drop-kicking optimistically from the halfway line.

She had not Ruth Draper's trick of evoking every object she mentioned, a pair of scissors or a cake, balloons, a bunch of flowers. Ruth Draper, more expansive, slower, gave herself time for what someone called tactile mimicry. Joyce Grenfell was quicker, prepared to cut corners, to count on her listeners' responsiveness. She gave fewer clues than Ruth Draper did, though – if seldom elaborating – she did love the relevant irrelevance ('Well, they're not very nice, hormones'; 'I see his cuff go in the beet salad, but I dint say nothing'). Vocally, she was exact. For the rest, she gave us the essentials, as in a 'Max' cartoon. To look again at such speeches as these is to remember her stop-watch timing (Herbert Farjeon told her she should go down on her knees in gratitude for her sense of it), the curl and swerve of her voice, the clicking, rapping consonants:

[The wife of the Vice-Chancellor of an Oxbridge University]: 'Alas, one of the things of which I am not possessed is an *in*formal hat. I fear my hats tend to be rather purposeful.'

[A foreign visitor, possibly Dutch with a Scandinavian mother]: 'Is dis not a smeshing cocktail party? I am so fond for a cocktail party. I sink is so nice to say hello and goodbye quick, and to have little sings for eating is so gay. Is always quite noisy and nowhere for sitting.'

[At a meeting of the Ladies' Choral somewhere north of Birmingham]: 'You know, I was stood next to her at practice last week when we did "The Wild Brown Bee is my Lover". When we'd finished I said to her very tactfully, thinking she might like to take the hint, I said: "I wonder who it is stands out so among the altos?" and she said she hadn't noticed. Hadn't noticed!'

Not everyone, I suppose, may agree that in the last speech Joyce Grenfell's vowels were tilted like a swing-boat at the top of its rise. Still, that was how I heard them. It was her own form of heightened speech, and she would be the last to express surprise at anything anybody heard. Did she not once seek the music's message, the rhythms of the earth and sea and sky? And what did she hear? 'You're a horse,' said the music, 'a great white horse.'

She could create so much so quickly that many of us wanted her in a play. She never yielded, though when she was eight she did impersonate a starving Burgher of Calais, followed at her next school by a truncated First Lord (*As You Like It*), and much later (at R.A.D.A.) by a singing dairymaid in a mob-cap. Sadly, this was the end. Films would be different: Miss Gossage, in the helter-skelter of *The Happiest Days of Your Life*, walking as if she were on a trampoline, and the police-sergeant in a games-mistress's gym-slip during something from St Trinian's. Otherwise, we have only the wistful pleasure of thinking what she might have played in the theatre. Not the older classics (possibly Helena in *A Midsummer Night's Dream*). But I can certainly imagine her as Miss Dyott, in Pinero's farce, *The Schoolmistress*, entering with a head under her arm and confiding: 'It is an embarrassing thing to break a bust in the house of comparative strangers.' Or possibly as the New England lady in a wig in some version of *Martin Chuzzlewit*: 'Mind and matter glide swift into the vortex of immensity. Howls the sublime and softly sleeps the calm Ideal, in the whispering chambers of Imagination.' Unfortunately, a very small part.

No: Joyce Grenfell chose the excitement, the ordered chaos, of revue, or of her own programmes where she could crowd the stage as she wished and slip into the songs that were so close a partnership with Richard Addinsell. Her voice might be frail. Never mind: she liked to sing, and she knew just what she could do with her own lyrics, though some of us may hear her more acutely as what used to be called a diseuse. A slightly alarming word, it invites comparison with Ruth Draper, Joyce Grenfell's distant relation and courtesy 'aunt'. Fuel here for students of heredity. Moreover, Joyce Grenfell's mother could imitate any accent and – in the style of the Draper 'Slovak Lullaby', *'Fleschne buva drub sorga'* – produce a variety of other sounds that passed for the real thing.

Everything that the splendidly redoubtable Ruth Draper did – she preferred to be known as a 'character actress' – was on a wider scale. Thinking of her sketches as dramas ('Three Women and Mr Clifford' for one) she had an architect's care for precise form, whereas Joyce Grenfell used a personal shorthand that caught her people in a few, often reiterated, verbal hieroglyphs. These were fortified by her ear for speech rhythms, by her joy in the absurd, and by the White Queen's gift for believing half-a-dozen impossible things before breakfast. Unlike the White Queen, she would tell us what they were. 'My grandmother's own particular interest,' said the Vice-Chancellor's Wife with exquisite articulation (if troubled by the letter 'r'), 'was in the world of very small mammals ... Yes, isn't it interesting? She had a long and very close relationship with a small red squirrel – yes, indeed, with a bushy tail ... She was convinced that this small red squirrel was in fact the reincarnation of a much-loved cousin, who had been gathered at an earlier date.' (The last five words are pure Grenfell.)

Somehow I cannot imagine Ruth Draper with those squirrels. A majestic artist, she could seem after the sixth or seventh hearing to lack Joyce Grenfell's steadily spontaneous, wide-eyed, generous pleasure in the rediscovery and idiosyncrasy of her people: always a Grenfell cast appeared to be fresh and buoyant. 'I can call spirits from the vasty deep' boasted Glendower. 'But will they come when you do call for them?' said Hotspur. We know that Ruth Draper's were in the wings, instantly on call. Joyce Grenfell's also, but she never took them for granted.

Joyce Grenfell knew about the young ('I used to scribble a bit ... Oh no, not love poems, more things like Spring, and Flowers ... and Death'), and she could have shown the garden with anyone. She was not a dowager. A gentle satirist, she seldom played against her audience as Ruth Draper did so surely with Mrs Clifford ('The cold, tired voice of unconcealed bore-

dom and fatigue'). And Lally Tullett's old friend who rocked on
the porch of a house in Virginia, as Ruth Draper's woman had
done in Maine, was not among her compelling parts: we knew
the woman without sharing her world as we did with most of
the others for whom Joyce Grenfell collected the show-piece
clichés and the richest accents: a party collected over the years,
the Edwardian hostess, the 'lady writer', the American mother
and Shelley's poem ('Byshe doesn't mean a thing, dear. It's his
name. His mother was probably a Miss Bysshe'), the Old Thyme
dancers ('Still it has to be, Some ladies dance together, One of
them is me'), the voices matched unerringly to Tufnell Park,
Pont Street, Bloomsbury, Godalming, and – birthplace unknown
– the Dutch-Scandinavian we have met before. This was the
woman who knew enough English to get it all wrong and to
express herself in the tones of a charmingly sibilant woodpecker:
'I am for bringing her a little gift horse. Is a chipple chopper. . . .
O dis is a little gedget knife for cutting up celery. I sink she vill
find him most useless.' She goes on her way remembering 'dis
little cat was sneezing in rhythm to de music of a Brahms. He
is not sneezing for Mozart, not for Beethoven, Shostakovich,
Chopin. No, no, only Brahms, and ven you vas going to de piano
dis little cat vas for sneezing. Oh, you have no piano and no
little cat? Oh, so sad.'

Only begin to quote the scripts, and you go on quoting, always
summoning the appropriate voice (such as the 'unlocalised accent
of great daintiness' for 'Useful and Acceptable Gifts') that is
tricky to score on paper. Joyce Grenfell had an almost infallible
Professor Higgins ear for complex variation in accent, a natural
ear trained further during her time with J. L. Garvin as the
Observer critic of radio. It is a medium in which the most
trivial speeches can be burnished, and a pebble that has looked
like nothing but a pebble is powdered suddenly with glinting mica.
Obviously she was happy on radio herself. When she first entered
the theatre there was premature worry that she might lose herself among the intricacies and condescend to stage Cockney –
rather in the way of an old repertory hand who used to misplace

an aspirate with painful labour. Nobody should have worried for a moment about Joyce Grenfell and Shirl's girl friend who was bred in radio and went on to the stage. One thinks of her on a night when the Big Wheel stuck and left her aloft with a Teddy-boy – label for the period – who, far from being an enthralling talker, was as curt as Mr Padge of hallowed memory. Shirl's girl friend had a properly crushing comment. 'Ta for the chat!' she said. She and various boy friends were always in trouble. It was a shame, I think, that they muddled the date of the costume buffet and dance at Brixton; if they had known they need not have gone all that way by bus and trolley on a wet night, wearing proper Chinese costumes – kimonos, chrysanths, fans and opium-pipes.

That was one of the groups. She was invariably at ease with the groups, not in the stippled detail of Ruth Draper, but in her own swift notation. Take the 'somewhere north of Birmingham' committee in Mrs Hailestone's front room, the telly full on at first, but not for long, and everyone – or nearly everyone – assembled, Mrs Brill, Mrs Culch, Mrs Pell, Mrs Hailestone, of course, May, and the chairman. Mrs Slope had sent an apology. So had Miss Heddle. And Lady Widmore tele-graphed: 'Alas cannot be with you devastated.' 'Can't come' interpreted the chairman curtly, getting down to important business – how to remove one unsuitable voice from the choir before the next festival. A pity that the owner of the voice should have founded the choir, but in Joyce Grenfell's world these things did happen. The chairman, her speech honed to a gleam-ing sharpness – the edge of an executioner's axe – drew the committee about her, and we felt more than a little sorry for the victim, an absent Mrs Codlin, and for May, the incompetent dogsbody, one of the meek who would not inherit the earth: she was due for a long talk before Madam Chairman mounted her bike.

That was one Grenfell group. Another was from a more-or-less continental-style revue with 'fairly disinterested ladies' chanting 'Fiesta! Fiesta!' in tones of modified rapture. Yet another, an Artists' Room crush after a recital, with the pianist receiving members of his audience, the philistines, the dead-heads, the merely moronic ('Beethoven does go on so'). Better still were certain of the conversation-pieces for two, such as that – made by its timing – when the friend-to-tea, poor soul, could not slot in a word because her hostess was so bothered by the iron in the kitchen, a picture awry, and the cushion rumpled. Here Joyce Grenfell, with a voice that com-bined miraculously wind-in-the-rigging and an absent-minded graciousness, might have been illustrating a pronouncement of St John Ervine (mildest of men in private, gruffest in print): 'Restless interruption, inability to sustain an idea to the end, is commoner among women than men.' We do not forget a moment when the hostess, her eyes alive with simulated interest, exclaimed vaguely: 'How is poor Ethel? I was *terribly* worried when I heard she was tap-dancing again ... Here's a pretty box, made by a Zulu.' We would never have imagined that the word 'Zulu' had so many vowels; they ululated like the *roucoulement* of an over-anxious wood-pigeon.

This was the kind of thing that puzzled Nellie Wallace. Generally, I was less persuaded by Joyce Grenfell's more serious sketches, the pathos, occasional stiff upper-lip, cumulative wist-fulness. Not that she did not feel them. But they were harder to transmit – 'Three Brothers', say, or the very different 'Lally Tullett', or a mother and grandmother seeing off the emigrants on the boat-train. Sometimes touching on the night, they are a little uncomfortable in remembrance. Personally, I was relieved when the gleam returned to Joyce Grenfell's eye; when the understanding mother was sweetly unsure about Harriet and the middle-aged Portuguese conjuror; or the children's writer confessed archly that her stories wrote themselves when she was in her little hidey-hole; or the faintly astringent Vice-Chancellor's Wife observed to her interviewer, a Mr Wimble: 'I expect you have *Locksley Hall* by heart, and I very much wish I had.' Line upon line recur: 'I like a nice scream when it's for pleasure'; 'a good problematical love-tale is nice' (a fond caress on 'problematical'); or the soothing Scandinavian-Dutch response, 'I am sensational, senk you.'

She was, above all, an undistracted hostess and a superb story-teller who rarely seemed to tell the same story twice. In what is now a primeval age people would complain oddly that she was wrong to take her party-pieces into the strictly guarded preserve of the professional theatre. Very soon indeed the cry waned. She never failed to reach the stage as if she were doing it all for fun: no hint of the metallic method of one renowned English comedienne, so composed technically, every hair, syllable, movement, in place, that she became an idol over more than thirty years. For all that technique, her eyes could be as blank as the empty sockets of a Roman statue. Joyce Grenfell looked through the eyes of her characters: the housewife who found fulfilment with Glad in the 'loverly laundrette', the Countess of Coteley ('decorative but dumb'), or a Victorian beauty worried that she could stir anyone but George du Maurier:

> I seem to delight each pre-Raphaelite, Mr Holman Hunt
>   takes me to lunch;
> I've been done in half-tones by Sir Edward Burne-Jones,
>   but I've never appeared in *Punch*.

She would gaze at the audience like a mild neighbourly starling, or with the mischievous glee of a Noël Coward schoolgirl who sang 'That is the end of the News' in *Sigh No More*; command a house (in words for another player long ago) like the head-lamps of a car turning the corner of a night-dark road; or just smile benignly while keeping rock-still: she was never a fidget. Her eyes were eloquent in the nursery school where free activity meant half an hour of turmoil with the tots, George was doing what he shouldn't, Hazel had her finger in the keyhole like the Dutch child who plugged the dike, and the teacher's voice could modulate from the implausibly saccharine – a special tone for very small children – to the helplessly appealing ('Who is making that buzzing noise?') and the practically distraught: 'I saw you deliberately put that paintbrush up Dolores' little nostril' (in the last vowel an age of agony).

I see that I have mentioned at random Shakespeare, O'Casey, Farjeon, Bernard Shaw, Pinero, Ivor Brown, Dickens, Lewis Carroll, St John Ervine, Mr Padge and Ruth Draper. While there is time I would like to add the seventeenth-century James Howell – until recently a stranger – who wrote 'Some hold translations not unlike to be/The wrong side of a Turkey tapestry.' Undeniably the second line has a Grenfell note (perhaps the Vice-Chancellor's wife). Lined up with these associates – and no doubt a trifle bothered – are the members of the Grenfell society: Mrs Hailestone, Mrs Codlin, and the unnamed Chairman (joining in 'My Bosom is a Nest'), Mr Molder, Mrs Finley, Lionel Pilgrim, Lady Hetting, Mrs Tiverton (who has to dance the man in the Valse Valeta), Mr Wimble, Mrs Ingstone, Ethel, Glad, Harriet, Dolores; Norm's friend Walter who gets Shirl to whistle the echo in that Elizabethan rarity entitled 'Friar Balsam's Repeat'; and, again, the Vice-Chancellor's Wife who would rather have people than animals – 'people for talking to and inventing safety-pins and playing Mozart'. Many others: all splendidly oblivious of every kind of stage revolution, Theatres of Protest and Cruelty and the Absurd, mayfly fashions, teasy skirmishing.

They, and their voices or their tingling silence, are guests at the Grenfell party: a grand reunion for one actress – the amused eyes beneath the fringe, the poise, the mobile mouth, the fertilising eagerness – in herself a whole cry of players during a lifetime since that night in the Adelphi: 'Madam President, Fellow Institute Members ... Be *bold* about it! You can make great sprays of lupes, or delphs.' What, as fellow-guests, can we say now? In gratitude and admiration, 'It's very good to see you in our midst,' or 'Sensational, senk you,' or, very simply– and in spite of a bewildered Nellie Wallace all those years ago – 'Ta for the chat!'

JOYCE GRENFELL
A Little Talk by Fern Brixton

Look here, can I speak freely? Good.

Well, here goes.

I'm not at all happy about the world. Something's got to be done about it, and if the High-ups aren't going to do it, then it's up to us Ordinary Mortals to pitch in and see what we can do. Agreed? Right.

I live in the country – not a thousand miles from Stonehenge, if you must know – and I like nothing better than to fling on an old coat and an old pair of clod-hoppers and trudge. Now when you trudge you get to pondering, and I'm quite a bit of a ponderer. I trudge and ponder with old Flatfoot – she's a black cocker spaniel friend of mine – and we go for miles. Well, the other afternoon we got in after a longish trudge, and I'd been searching the old grey matter for some sort of solution to the world's problems, and I was hungry. So was old Flatfoot. I fixed her a meal, and then I boiled me a goodly brown egg, and, as I spooned it into my earthenware eggcup, I suddenly saw something. And what I saw was this:

It's not right to eat eggs.

I know this is a small thing – a very small thing – but big things are made up of lots and lots of small things, and it seems to me that if we can put the small things right we've begun the job.

I looked at this egg, and it was absolutely lovely. Pinkish brown – completely smooth and really pretty perfect – and I thought to myself: 'What right have you to this egg? You didn't lay it. All you did was feed its mother and then take her egg away from her – steal it. It might have come from Mrs Henny-penny, or Florence, or Snowdrop. They're all good hens and splendid layers, and they are all good friends of mine, too.

I was appalled. Here was I, year after year doing this wrong thing – and I think this is the point – NOT KNOWING IT WAS WRONG. Not, that is, until this moment of blinding revelation. I was tremendously shaken.

At first I thought, I can't – I mustn't eat you. But then, I thought none of the girls would want to take back a three-minute boiled egg, so, very quietly and with a great sense of occasion, I ate my last egg.

It was delicious.

But it was WRONG.

It was not mine to eat – not, that is, in the eyes of nature. It belonged to one of the girls, and I must never, never knowingly do this wrong again.

I think I know what you are thinking: What are hens FOR if they aren't there to give us eggs?

I have given this a good deal of thought, and I don't know the answer. But this I do know. Eggs belongs to their mothers. And that is why I'm so glad to have this little talk with you – to open your eyes as mine have been opened, and with this small beginning, who knows what great things we may not do?

For those of you who keep hens I must warn you: there are problems. The eggs do pile up rather. And, of course, the hens don't always understand what is going on. But I do believe that in their hearts they must know we are trying to do what's right. And it is not right to eat eggs.

JOYCE GRENFELL

Daughter and Mother

Oh Mummy, you don't understand. I've been thinking an awful lot about you and Daddy, now that you're both so old. Well, you're forty. Well, thirty-eight, then. Anyway, quite old – and you don't understand life any more. You see, Mummy, you married Daddy when you were frightfully young and you've been perfectly happy ever since, so no wonder you don't understand, because you've never suffered. I think it's rather pathetic really. Well, you don't like noise, and you think people ought to eat regular meals, and you don't understand about Art or anything. You and Daddy both think that if a person's going to do anything, they've got to learn *how* to do it, and then to work and work *hard*.

That's a frightful thing to say.

You see, you don't understand. Look – it's miles harder *not* to work than to work. Eric Witzler says that it's absolutely wrong to work, work is the coward's way out. And he says a creative artist must learn to starve if necessary.

No, he's the one who finished the cheese at supper on Sunday.

I suppose you think it's easy to paint a picture entirely solid blue. Well, it isn't. It takes hours and hours of concentration and discipline. It took Eric three whole days before he ever *touched* the canvas, and absolutely *everyone* thinks it's the most exciting picture they ever saw in their whole lives. Well – everyone. Well – Esmond and Peggy and me.

Eric has such a tragic life. Well, he has to live at home with his family, and do you know he isn't allowed to play the gramophone or the radio after ten o'clock at night. You see, you *don't* understand. You and Daddy think it's awful to have the gramo-

82

phone on all the time. But everyone up at the Universities do all their most complicated maths and science and that sort of thing with the radio and gramophones full on the whole time. Because it's the *only* way to concentrate.

And another thing, you think it's awful when I lie on the sofa and telephone someone for an hour.

But it's normal, Mummy.

I don't know how to say this without hurting your feelings, but you know last Saturday at Uncle Jim's? Well, you know the way we all played tennis? Well, I don't think you and Daddy ought to have beaten people so much younger than yourselves. George Pasby and Eleanor Dill are supposed to be frightfully good, and you kept sending them balls they couldn't take, and they didn't like it. And lobbing is frightfully old-fashioned.

And I don't think you and Daddy ought to dance so sort of – well – enthusiastically – like you did at the Wilsons'. I mean, everyone was staring at you. You looked as if you were enjoying it.

Well, you ought not to of.

Look, Mummy, don't feel you've got to keep up with us. You've had a frightfully long life, and you must be tired. Are you going out tonight?

I just wondered. Nothing. I only asked.

Well, I wondered if you were going to wear your new jacket? Well, I mean, if you didn't actually want it, perhaps I could sort of borrow it.

Well, I just thought – Mummy, you're laughing at me!

JOAN DE BETHEL

Dressing for the Stage

People often say of Joyce that she was a very good professional amateur; but she was not so much an amateur as a craftsman. She had no dazzling technique that she could switch on in a professional actor's way. Each performance was a 'one-off' piece, rather like a potter's, or artist's. It was put together in a 'one-off' way. It evolved.

During *Tuppence Coloured* I showed some designs to Laurier Lister, who liked them and said he would remember me when he did his next revue. I thought no more about it, as this is the usual thing you are told. But he did remember, and asked me to do some designs for *Penny Plain* in 1951. And so I designed some of the sets and costumes for Joyce's shows; but this really meant the period costumes – Victor Stiebel did the modern dresses. Joyce herself hatched up her character clothes. Luckily we both had the same approach: what would that particular person be wearing, character-wise? Where would she have got it?
the same approach: what would that particular person be wearing, character-wise? Where would she have got it?

When a revue first starts the management hires all the costumes and props for all but the really safe fixed numbers, as during the tour, before coming to London, a lot of alterations are made, and some numbers are dropped or replaced. We had one in *Penny Plain*, a sort of Healthy Country Dancing group doing a rather boring ethnic dance, all with slab-faces, white shirts, white trousers for the men, and white blouses and coloured skirts for the ladies. This was thought to need brightening up for London, but as cheaply as possible, due to the expenses incurred on the tour.

'They would be wearing something they had all made themselves,' said Joyce.

So we got some white cardigans – I think from Marks and Spencer's – and Joyce sat in her dressing-room embroidering 'bold, bright patterns in coloured wools' all over them. She was very good indeed at needlework and was seldom without some needlepoint. She got through quite a bit in the way of rugs while waiting about for her calls in the film studios.

Also in *Penny Plain* was a number about 'Maud' (Tennyson's 'Come into the Garden, Maud') which Joyce did with the late Julian Orchard – his first ever revue. We wanted a dress based roughly on a Sargent portrait Joyce had of her grandmother, a white dress with a striped bodice, in the 1880s; but we put the dress back into the Tennyson period, when the crinoline had gone out but the bustle had not yet come in – more like the 1870s. A 'sewing lady' made the dress, all in white organdie, a lovely soft material, but hopeless for theatre work, where costumes get a fair bashing. In no time it was limp and floppy; it hung rather than stood out. Joyce and I saw it for the first time at Southsea where the revue opened. We were both disappointed, but finance was tight, as money had not started to come in. The skirt needed remaking altogether with more petticoats of a stiffer material underneath – twice the amount of material, and not organdie. Joyce solved the situation by paying for it herself.

For *Requests the Pleasure* we had two very good costumiers, Carl Bonn and Colin Mackenzie. Carl was a wonderful cutter and fitter, and Colin excelled in hand-made detail. It was their first show in London. At the time they were somewhere off the Fulham Road working from their flat. Joyce was living over the sweetshop in the King's Road, and I was just round the corner in the Little Boltons. So it was very convenient for us all. Carl and Colin went on to work for Covent Garden, the Royal Ballet, the National Theatre and television.

One of the hazards of costume-making is girls who wear comfy old bras for rehearsals when the costume fittings are done, then go out and buy a brand-new uplift bra for the first night – which, of course, alters the whole fit of the costume. Joyce arrived at one fitting, for a tight-fitting Edwardian ball dress, in what she would have herself described in one of her monologues as 'one of those warm vests, you know, the sort with built-up shoulders, and nice and long – and long warm knickers to go with it'. It was winter. She apologised for this, as she had not been able to get home and change after her previous engagement. 'Still,' she added, 'as my mother used to say, as long as it's all clean and decent you've nothing to worry about.'

In the opening number in *Penny Plain* the whole cast came down front in a row, Joyce in the centre. Rehearsals were on, and Laurier Lister, sitting in the stalls at the St Martin's Theatre, said, 'You *must* spread out more – this way.' They repeated the entry several times, still not getting centre. 'It's all right, Laurier,' said Joyce, 'I can see a brass stud thing right down there. It's on the centre, so I can come down to that.'

There were audible winces behind me – 'Awful amateurism!' and 'brass stud thing!' from someone who had less experience of the theatre than Joyce. But, after all, if there *was* a convenient 'brass stud thing' in the centre, and it *was* visible, why not use it? I think it was something to do with the electric dips, but I doubt whether the person who made the remark knew this either.

Joyce had a family, or household, approach to her numbers, which was shared with the audience. It was a household they were all familiar with, the irritating things and the funny things. It was never 'theatrical', and the homely atmosphere extended to the rehearsals. The rest of the cast had had a full training at a theatre school: movement, voice production, singing projection, and all the rest that Joyce never had, except for one term at R.A.D.A. Practically all her numbers were solos, so she did not have to work with the rest of the cast, except when they were all on the stage for a production number, the first-act finale, the opening number and the closing number. Conversations in her dressing-room tended to be about the fact that she had taken down her curtains, and whether she should wash them or take them to the cleaners. They were nicer washed, but the difficulty was getting them dry. Or such things as the price of daffodils being high due to the late spring – the everyday things one tended to talk about when one went to tea with someone. It was this atmosphere that was constantly there when Joyce was.

WILLIAM BLEZARD

The Other Side of the Keyboard

I first met Joyce in 1954, when she expanded her theatrical appearances from one or two solo items in revue to a complete show. This was *Joyce Grenfell Requests the Pleasure*, shared by three brilliant young dancers: Beryl Kaye, Irving Davies and Paddy Stone, and an ensemble of eight instrumentalists, of which I was the pianist, and had the new experience of directing professional musicians from the keyboard. The whole thing was put together by Laurier Lister. After a five-week pre-London tour, which opened in Cambridge on 26 April, the show was knitting together nicely, but we hadn't the slightest idea what sort of reception audience or critics would give it when we came to the Fortune Theatre on 2 June to start a West End season. To our great joy the notices were uniformly rapturous. I never read such unqualified enthusiasm for an opening night.

We ran for eight months, eventually moving to the St Martin's Theatre, where a hideous hired piano was hastily replaced after one agonising night by the lucky purchase of a Bechstein upright from Harrods' Piano Sale. The show ran till February 1955. After a welcome holiday we began another tour, in which Aberdeen stands out in my memory as one of the only two places in the world that seemed unresponsive to Joyce's charm. The other was a religious college in Pennsylvania where attendance at the concert had been made compulsory for the students.

Joyce was a tower of strength, never allowing the problems of a new theatrical venture to worry her. She was a serene central figure who always remained unruffled and optimistic. This was wonderfully beneficial, for when the star of a show radiates calm and good humour everyone can settle down free of stress and strain.

I had good reason to be grateful for this during our second provincial tour. We had been moving from town to town, each theatre with a different starting time, and that week we were at Manchester Opera House. After a matinée performance I had gone straight to the Central Library and become totally immersed in a book. Gradually it dawned on me that I should be getting back to the theatre for the evening performance. I set off with, I thought, enough time to change and be ready to enter the orchestra pit at 7.30, but when I reached the Opera House I was amazed to see that there wasn't a person in sight, only a large poster, which said 'Evenings at 7'. It was then 7.15. I hurtled myself round to the stage door past a frenzied stage manager and heard a strange pianoless version of the overture being bravely executed by the rest of the players. I leapt into the saddle, so to speak, received a round of applause from a remarkably patient audience, and brought the music to a halt at the first possible cadence point, so that the curtain could go up.

Joyce, apparently, had come on stage, and explained that the musical director would be a little late, 'but we're going to make a start', adding, as she retreated off-stage, 'You're not supposed to have seen me.' This happy inspiration won the audience's hearts, and got over a very awkward situation. All she said to me afterwards was 'You'll remember this occasion for the rest of your life.' And I have. Needless to say I rushed out as soon as possible and bought her a huge bunch of flowers, presenting them penitentially with a quotation from the song 'There is a lady sweet and kind', with additional words to fit the occasion.

Joyce was never a stickler for theatrical tradition. She played things by instinct, and her reaction was usually right. Her motto was 'Whatever happens, never show unease or embarrassment on stage, and then the audience won't feel any.'

In Melbourne in 1963 there was an occasion which I described in a letter home:

A sudden tremendous hailstorm during the performance hit the metal roof with such force that we could hardly hear each other. Having just started a song, Joyce stopped, and, after a brief comment on the situation, swung into 'Oh what a beautiful ...' substituting the word 'evening' for 'morning'. I joined in with an accompaniment, and as we were getting to the end of this well-known tune from *Oklahoma*, at 'everything's going my way', the hail suddenly stopped as if someone had pulled a switch. The performance then continued without any further interruption. A friend of mine who was present at the time almost persuaded himself that it was all prearranged, so felicitously did she cope with the situation. (How does one prearrange a hailstorm, though?)

When *Joyce Grenfell Requests the Pleasure* went to New York, the American Musicians' Union wouldn't allow me as a non-member to conduct the show, and the accomplished jazz pianist George Bauer took over my duties. It was also with him that Joyce first tried out her one-woman show on tours of the United States. He provided a spot in each half to allow her a moment's respite and time to change her costume. Thus a simple formula evolved with the minimum of accessories and back-stage help; with a stage-manager to set up a lighting plot, a chair, a small table, a sofa and a grand piano with an adjustable stool, the show was ready to go. It could be moved about the world with the greatest of ease. The pattern was set.

In 1957 Joyce performed her one-woman show for the first time in this country. After playing-in visits to Dublin, Newcastle and Glasgow we began a four-week season at the old Lyric Theatre, Hammersmith. It was a great success, and I was very happy to be part of this new pattern which established Joyce as one of those rare performers who virtually single-handed could captivate an audience for two hours.

In 1959 we made a long trip to Australia to begin a thirteen-week season in Sydney at the old Phillip Street Theatre. The building was owned by the Workers Education Association, which had also rented out premises above and below the auditorium. One Saturday night a thunderous noise suddenly started above us. Joyce simply had to stop, because no one could hear her properly. An action-packed film was being shown upstairs; and only after someone had been persuaded to turn down the volume to a tolerable level was Joyce able to continue.

During this long season she adopted a very disciplined lifestyle. There were eight performances a week, with gruelling Fridays and Saturdays of two performances each evening. On these two days Joyce was never seen until forty-five minutes before the first show was due to begin. On other days she would accept only morning engagements and luncheon invitations. The afternoon was sacrosanct: then she would rest and go over her words. After the evening performance she went straight home to the flat. As a result she was always able to give her best at every show. This rigid routine was broken only once, when Reggie arrived in Sydney towards the end of the run; his plane was four hours late but she still went out to the airport to meet him at 2.30 in the morning.

After the exhausting Fridays and Saturdays, Joyce was ready for a well-earned day off, and on most Sunday evenings we had a meal at her flat, usually followed by a game of Scrabble, which she had introduced me to on the outward flight between Singapore and Djakarta. They were fiercely-fought games, if only on my part, because it was hard to offer her enough of a challenge. I found a triumphant note in a letter home: 'Beat Joyce by one point.' On these get-togethers Joyce would do the cooking herself. Her maxim was 'Never do anything that can't be prepared in a few minutes, and stick to good simple ingredients.' The result was always excellent.

The show had been running smoothly for several weeks when I wrote home on 21 August: 'Poor Joyce has lost nearly all her singing voice, and this has entailed a hurried change of programme with all vocal numbers spoken. So I am the only one who sings at the moment.' This was when I imploringly sang 'Come into the Garden, Maud', and she replied, 'Maud's not coming into the garden, let that be clearly understood!' 'P.S: I've just played "Woman on the Bus" six keys lower, which enabled Joyce to sing a few Rex Harrison notes!"

Sunday, 22 August: 'Joyce has hardly sung a note since Wednesday. I've been transposing things on a sliding scale. Her present range, which is about five notes, shifts upwards from day to day. Foot-mikes have been installed, and she's managing very well by some miracle. The weather may be responsible for the trouble, as it is treacherous at this time of year and throat complaints are very prevalent. One moment it will be boiling hot, the next quite chilly.'

25 August: 'Still changing keys, "Voice of Joyce" coming back, but isn't yet in the right place. We're still some four keys down. And so on until gradually it returned to normal.'

Joyce's normal vocal range would vary considerably, depending on the song. She didn't usually like to go higher than the second E flat above middle C, but when taking off someone with a high voice, she could miraculously sing stunningly high notes as clear as a bell, which she would have thought impossible in other songs. She was very good at characterisation, as in the 'Songs My Mother Taught Me'. These obviously struck a deep chord, going back to her childhood. Her voice, while not of great power, had a very pleasing quality, except on rare occasions when a note was a shade under pitch, probably because she had not complete vocal control, certainly not because of any lack of ear. It is remarkable how well Joyce could change quickly from speech to song, considering the enormous demands she made on her vocal cords in varying the character of her voice.

Her musicality was shown in her amazing ability to improvise. During warm-ups before the performance we would often extemporise entire songs in the style of: German *Lieder*, French *chansons* or a typically English Roger Quilter. I can't describe quite how this was done, but it was certainly great fun to improvise accompaniments to her spontaneously invented words and melody. I have only one tape of poor technical quality to remind me how brilliant she was at it.

She did not do as much ad-libbing in an actual show as one might think. There was always a set text, every word written by Joyce herself, but felicitous variations and additions would creep in from time to time, especially when she was feeling happy and relaxed with her audience, and then we would frantically rack our brains afterwards to remember just what new remark had popped out during the show, so that it would be incorporated into the text.

Outside the theatre she could improvise off-the-cuff with masterly effect. Once we were invited to a society luncheon, with no idea what to expect. We were shown into a large room full of middle-aged ladies in extraordinary hats. A retired army officer, one of the only four men present, met us at the door and showed us to our seats at a table on a platform facing the assembly. They had already started their meal on their knees, and by the time we were served they had all finished, and could concentrate on watching us munching triangular sandwiches, home-made scones and a large cream cake. When we had finished, the retired military gentleman stood up and made a long jingoistic peroration, followed by a eulogy of Joyce, then of our promoter, and finally of me. When at last he sat down, Joyce stood up and got this rather stuffy audience going, asking questions, which she answered with marvellous fluency and much wit. It was a splendid performance, and with her instinctive sense of timing she sat down at exactly the right moment.

Joyce has told of her many tours in her book, *In Pleasant Places*. Looking back it all seems to have been wonderfully successful. Of course there were occasional snags, as when Joyce's radio mike picked up police messages or when the bagpipes, in Auckland, New Zealand, played on Friday nights at a hall far too close to the theatre for comfort. Personally I find distance lends enchantment to these instruments – for example, the piper on one mountain and the listener on another. But there was one exception. The very last performance Joyce and I did together was at Windsor Castle at the Queen's personal invitation (a Royal Command I suppose one could call it). We were also delighted to be invited, together with sixty-eight others, to the annual Waterloo Dinner beforehand. As it came to a close we heard the distant sound of pipes gradually coming nearer, as the pipers marched down the corridors and finally strode into the Waterloo Chamber. They circled the candle-lit table with their kilts swinging magnificently in time to the music. The total effect was electrifying – especially when they passed behind one's chair, and the volume was deafening. It was quite unforgettable. This splendid occasion ended Joyce's performing career, apart from a radio broadcast and a double L.P. that we did together. Had I known it at the time it would have tinged the occasion with sadness.

Joyce was infinitely more than a professional associate. She was a very kind friend, always personally concerned with me and my family. She gave me a sense of security and confidence over a long spell of time, for which I am deeply grateful. With her energetic endeavour and great talent Joyce was always so cheerful and positive about life, and never moody. She was steadfast, dependable and true.

JOHN WARD

Two Letters

[We asked John Ward if he would contribute one of his cele-brated illustrated letters to this book, and with his usual generosity he provided two. The first is a newly-illustrated version of a letter he wrote in 1969 after Joyce had given a concert at Canterbury in support of the Stour Music Festival with which he was concerned. But then he felt that there was much that he had failed to say. So he dashed off the second letter in case we might prefer to use it instead. We have, of course, put in both of them.]

Dear, dear Joyce

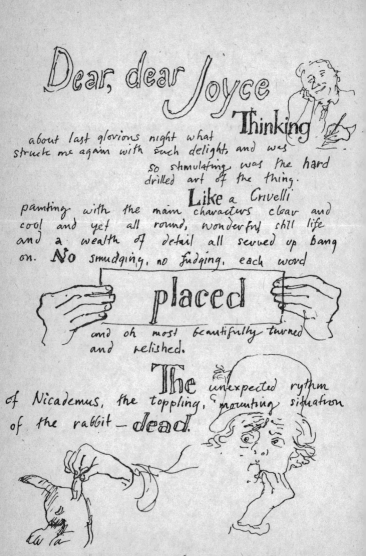

Thinking about last glorious night what struck me again with such delights and was so stimulating was the hard drilled art of the thing.

Like a Crivelli painting with the main characters clear and cool and yet all round, wonderful still life and a wealth of detail all served up bang on. **No** smudging, no fudging, each word

placed

and oh most beautifully turned and relished.

The unexpected rythm of Nicademus, the toppling, mounting situation of the rabbit — **dead.**

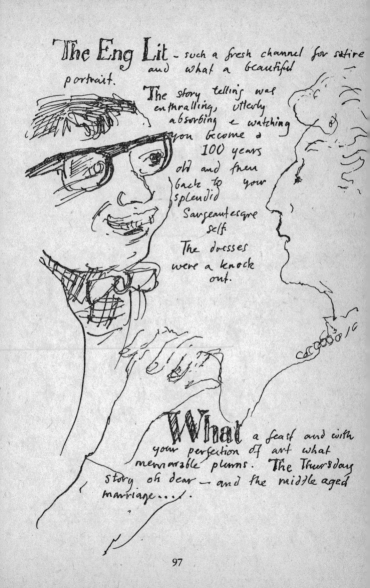

The Eng Lit - such a fresh channel for satire and what a beautiful portrait.

The story telling was enthralling, utterly absorbing & watching you become a 100 years old and then back to your splendid Sargeantesque self

The dresses were a knock out.

What a feast and with your perfection of art what memorable plums. The Thursday story oh dear — and the middle aged marriage....

97

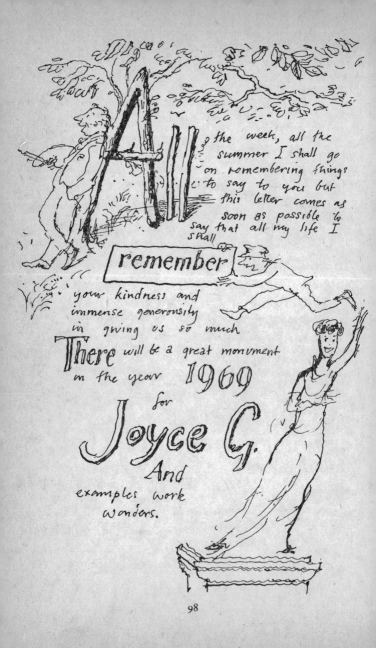

All the week, all the summer I shall go on remembering things to say to you but this letter comes as soon as possible to say that all my life I shall

remember

your kindness and immense generousity in giving us so much

There will be a great monument in the year 1969

for

Joyce G.

And examples work wonders.

Please thank Reggie
for coming — and love dear
Joyce, not only from me but
from everyone who packed
the hall last night.

Yours.

John

Dear Richard

You stab me to the heart. I'm

When a bill arrives, when a friend writes, when there is free paper & stamps — envelopes around then I can scribble away.

BUT —

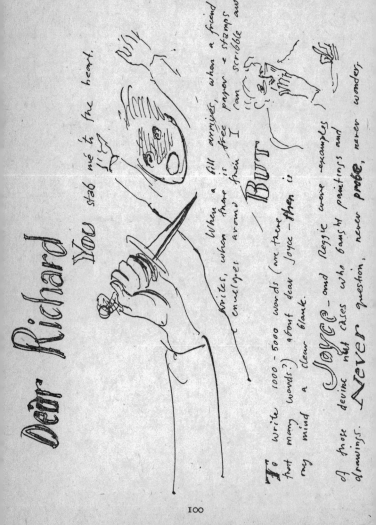

To write 1000 — 5000 words (are there that many words?) about dear Joyce — then is my mind a clear blank. **JOYCE** — and Reggie were examples of those devine nut cases who bought paintings and drawings. **Never** question, never **probe**, never wonder

Joyce Phipps, 1913

The Débutante

Joyce and Virginia

Joyce and Stephen Potter at work

The Pen Friend

The Actress

The Author with Joan Axell, Reggie
and Bert Axell twenty days before she died

WHY

people buy pictures just be thankful for the miracle
I met Joyce when I was drawing for Vogue
(a fascinating job after 6 years as a private soldier)

I think Joyce saw that, while I had
no way sharp eye for fashion I wasn't
adverse and to drawing pretty women. At that
time all students had in averted their
eyes when a pretty girl came by. We were
in generation seeking truth through
honesty & ugliness.
I was a Traitor

Flowers too, I
enjoyed drawing & so
dear Joyce asked me
to come & draw her.

She then lived over the
sweet shop & she set one
side of the table & I
sat the other — I in
the kitchen back & true
& she in the dining
room back & the dresser.

I drew away and as with all portraits one eye was OK the other a bit funny

first by rubbing & scraping & got it right and I drooled over her flowers and bits of china.

After that we were away and for nigh on 30 years she found sitters for me. Rossi, ma & Petcho, he Stype man at St Martins Theatre, her lovely pebbles in the portrait painters doors — friends, brought forth such lovely ripples which pond

You see she didn't ask for just a portrait head, so much of a person, particularly people she is fond of, lies in the set of their elbows or the way their knees touch their chins & in their knick knacks — their shortness, their fatness. **All this I** relished immensely.

Then, she too had a taste for watercolours between us that was that fond of sketching stools sitting on dabbling awing sketching afternoons in the manner of the old ladies who filled the art school at Stratford afternoons before one discovered that ART (where I first trained) — (such was I full of MEANING)

Joyce's

shrewd perception quickly spotted the fact that art is a very unsentimental commodity. That although it is laudable to wish & paint GREAT works unless one has the equipment the results can be pretty ridiculous. That very minor works can have a nobleness — a fishpaste pot full of primroses well painted can have a touch of Dido on a 6 foot canvas.

BUT
better by far to talk about the paint box, the paper, mud and weather the minute you get the wind on you

Gave tu paints off Art.

Joyce

backed her
fancies and hearers
wasn't I lucky to
have been one of them.

She needed out a
talent with the pleasure
& patience one picks out:
teeth after a good
dish of fish.

Some day

people will realise that
what is needed is the cultivation
of Patrons. Artists, like the rain & snow & spring you will always have
but ninety per cent of them need patrons who perceive that
where & how an artist will flourish, withand patrons we work
around wondering whether we are needed & too many of us stumbled
for want of care — wasn't I lucky to come across Joyce & Reggie!

JOYCE GRENFELL

Craftsmanship

When will it come again
The love of the job
Because of the job?
When will the hand regain
Its right to pride,
The task-tired fingers know
The pleasure of craft
Because of the craft?

Building with words, with stone,
With music, silk, with wood,
With paint, with line, with earth—
It is the doing that's good,
The giving birth.

JOYCE GRENFELL
Mrs A.

[*A description of Hester Alington, upon whose use of words Joyce based her favourite 'character', the Vice-Chancellor's Wife.*]

It is easier to say what Mrs A. didn't look like than to find an exact simile. She didn't look like a headmaster's wife. She didn't really look like a dean's wife, either. She was, of course, both.

If you came upon her isolated from her setting and family she might suggest a woman gifted for gardening – roses, I think – and highly skilled in domesticity. She looked like a mother, too; one with a light hand for pastry, but she said of herself: 'I don't suppose there is anyone in the world more at a loss when confronted with an egg.' She knew exactly what to do when confronted with a child. It wasn't for nothing that she headed the Mothers' Union.

I don't think I ever saw her hair looking as if it had been 'done'. I believe it used to be a wonderful Pre-Raphaelite red, but when I knew it it was a soft, pale colour, but an afterglow of the red remained in a faint way. She wore it piled up into a rather loosely baked bun. It never looked as if it would stay where it was for long, but I never saw it come down. She gave an impression of timelessness. She sat easy, as they say in the mountains of North Carolina. She was unhurried and gave one a sense of space.

I believe I have an observant eye, but try as I do I cannot remember what Mrs A. wore. I know she had timeless kind of clothes, longer than the fashion. I know she wore hats that went on her head and didn't perch. But so powerful was the essential being inside the clothes and the hats that they contributed little that is memorable.

She may not have been beautiful in terms of bone and complexion. Her face was broad, the cheeks high. Her eyes that I seem to remember as dark amber coloured, were deeply set. Her mouth was wide and mobile, and quick to smile. There emanated from her being a light, a warmth and a radiance that were entirely beautiful.

Seen from the point of view of one who had known her slightly since childhood and more closely in the last fifteen years of her life, she was a beloved friend and a very special person. She was individual in all she thought and said and did. She was an original.

I see her lying on the sofa in the great long-windowed room at the Deanery in Durham with its dark bluey greeny Chinese wallpaper patterned with lemon trees and white birds and pale flowers. She kept the telephone on the floor beside her and was working on a vast embroidered bed-cover that flowed across her knees. (The one I remember was being made for Giles.) It was one of those rare times between desk-work and a ceaseless stream of M.U. ladies and Cathedral wives and others demanding attention. Viola was playing the piano for her. A huge log fire blazed. Mrs A. put down her needle to listen, gave a huge sigh of satisfaction and said, meaning it literally: 'That was heavenly. More please.'

Some people's voices sound like strings. Hers was a combination of double bass and some deep woodwind. Her laugh was low and rich with a whisper of in-drawn breath to finish it off.

She did not go in for strong language, but 'Great Lack!' sufficed to relieve her feelings. She had a very individual sort of lisp. It added greatly when she emphasised, and she emphasised a lot in a completely natural way. To write down the stresses she made would make her utterances appear affected, and that was the last thing they were. They flowed out of her, unedited, inevitable and entirely unlike anyone else's.

Who else would have drawn attention in the same way to 'a

regrettable absence of essential stationery in the visitor's bath-room'? The question of expenses came up over some concert I was doing for her, and she wrote to say 'we must touch on the sordid topic of coin'.

There are so many quotations. This postcard sent to a shoe shop in Sloane Street was observed on the hall table by one of the family and memorised: 'Gently fussed over non-appearance of rather dim pair of shoes sent to you for mending.' Gently fussed was the exact description of the uneasy stirrings the non-appearance had aroused in her.

Just after the war she had a problem cook coping in the dark distances below the Deanery. She was as difficult as possible and probably a little mad. She would not speak a word to anyone except Mrs A. Silence ruled her days, and she ignored the other members of the staff, including Nanny, as if they were not there. Mrs A. called this behaviour 'That un-natural kink', and referred to the menace in the kitchen as 'The Thunderstorm'. (Put a little blur on to the 's' in thunderstorm and you will get the added rich rumble.)

In my diary for 1948 is an entry rejoicing at being in Durham. 'Mrs A. is very lame but in the most blessed spirits. The white poodle has been named Mu because it is a present from the M.U.' 'Mrs A. has been juggling with splendid sentences all day.' The Dean had a birthday and she gave him an enormous dictionary of quotations: 'This is probably quite useless and quite unwelcome.'

She telephoned at some length to Alec and Elizabeth and called them in turn 'Dear Lord' and 'Arc-Angel'.

Another year I came again with Viola Tunnard to Durham to do some more concerts for Mrs A., and one of them was to be held in the dining-room. At lunch that day she warned the Dean: 'Dear sir, at three o'clock this room will be entirely deplorable for tonight.'

It is difficult to put on paper the quality of greatness that Mrs A. had. Was it her vision of Heaven? This seemed to be constant and immediate. She recognised that the best in anyone was all that mattered, and she had an instant awareness of this truth in quite unlikely people. She had humility. She had humour. Above all she had a sense of joy. This was no surface thing but rather a deep-seated, golden reverberation that responded to items large and small, to miracles, to jokes, to affection, to illumination and the goodness of God. Her faith went beyond words. She gave it out, unconsciously, at all times.

She knew plenty of sorrow in her long life, but she had a wider view of life in its entirety than most of us and her courage and steadfastness went on undiminished.

My mother met an old man up in the mountains of North Carolina and they spoke of a mutual friend who had died: 'He never met a stranger,' said the old man. I was reminded of this when Elizabeth told me that Mrs A. said: 'I only once met a bore.' History does not relate the identity of this lone figure.

Mrs A. met few strangers. She was, as an Oxford undergraduate wrote of her, 'keen on Heaven', and this keenness caused her to create an atmosphere of enormous joy wherever she was. There never was anybody quite like her, and to have known her is riches indeed.

JOYCE GRENFELL

Sonnet

If ever I am rich enough to make
   Generous gestures let me hide my hand.
Let me give freely lest my giving take
   With it freedom. Not the frailest strand
Of obligation must go with my gift,
   Nor must the comfort glow of being kind
Be used to lend a foolish head a lift.
   Grant I may bring a clear and seeing mind
To work in wisdom, giving with a touch
   So light that never breath of power blow
Across the crystal of my sharing much
   That is lovely. Pray I may mark and know:
Beauty dies like linnet in a cage,
Beneath the bruising hand of patronage.

[1940]

VERILY ANDERSON

A Time to Weep
and a Time to Laugh

The family were discussing what they wanted to be when they grew up – a stage designer, an author, a gamekeeper, which is what the elder ones eventually became. The little ones, then about nine and eight, had other ideas.

'I want to live with Reggie,' was Janie's.

'And I want to *be* Reggie,' was Alex's.

'Then what are you going to do with Joyce?' elder sister Rachel enquired.

'Keep her, of course,' said Janie. ''Cos Joyce is the thing I want to be.'

I think they supposed that Joyce and Reggie spent all their spare time chasing each other round the trees in Kensington Gardens, as they had just been hilariously doing with Janie and Alex.

We all agreed that nothing would be more wonderful than actually *being* Joyce.

'Comic, kind, keen and clever.' Eddie had just got on to alliteration.

'And also very, very clean,' said Marian. 'She smells marvellously of absolutely nothing at all. No scent. No hairspray. All fresh.'

They were thinking of the flat. No mice (except when Janie took her own there). No half-eaten apples. No half-dead flowers. But always lots of little vases of wild ones. People brought them or sent them in tight bud, as we did later when we lived in the country.

'I think I won't wait,' Janie, ever impetuous, said. 'I'll be Joyce now.'

'And I'll be Reggie.'

It was the next best thing to it, luckily for them, to grow up under the all-embracing influence of the two most unselfish, generous, loving people we are ever likely to know.

The children started to put on some of Joyce and Reggie's clothes, a great many of which have come on to us over the years after relatively short lives with their original owners.

Joyce has never been anything like the same shape as me. She was always taller, longer-necked, less bosomy and never, like me, without a waist; and yet in some surprising way her dresses and suits, coats and trousers, underclothes and dressing-gowns have always fitted me. 'Your chubby contours take up the length, dear,' she explained in her Nanny voice. If they looked too silly on me she said so and put them back in her cupboard.

As for shoes, just over size 7, but not quite 7½, has been my lot since I left school, and an awkward lot too. It was also Joyce's. Because of it she became a compulsive shoe buyer, afraid to pass by any pair of shoes that fitted in case years went by before she found another. The result was she had so many pairs that she hardly wore them more than a few times, so that not only did I have good, well-made shoes chosen and bought for me, but also broken in from their first stiffness to perfect comfort. A great Joyce dodge has always been to stick little patches of adhesive leather on to any places inside her shoes where there might be the slightest space. 'How incwedably fortunate,' Joyce said in the well-articulated voice of her imaginary Vice-Chancellor's Wife who could not pronounce he *r*s, 'that our pedal extwemities are so agweably twinn spacedd.'

Eddie was a long time growing into Reggie's green tweed suit. He had progressed from a small cherubic choir boy to a still tichy terror of a teenager.

Since my own loudly screaming childhood, I have not been much of a weeper except, oddly enough, *at* Joyce and Reggie, not, I hasten to add, in anger. The times Joyce answered the telephone to explosive sobs during Eddie's adolescence were many. '*Two* black eyes this time.' 'No, they've stopped banging doors on each other's heads. It was an ordinary fight this time.' 'He just won't wash.' 'He hasn't changed his shirt for a week.' 'Caught smoking.' '*Drunk* with cider.' And finally '*Expelled* for long hair.' Considering Joyce neither smoked nor drank and had a particularly high standard of neatness, it may seem odd that she was the one in whom I confided. In theory she should have been shocked. In theory I wanted her and Reggie to see us all at our best, and yet they were the very people I turned to when we were all at our worse. In fact Joyce always gave the impression that there was nothing to worry about. Everybody was perfect really. Sometimes a little error crept in. Meanwhile Eddie started to grow, both upwards and good again.

Not long ago I jotted down in my diary, 'Eddie came down from the hide he has made high up in the fir tree to photograph squirrels (tempted with chocolated nuts) and Joyce measured herself against him and found herself, she said, "wanting by about half a head". When we got to the top of the wood she said, "I think I'm in love with Eddie," pause "aren't you?" '

Sometimes she said: 'Don't you *love* good people?' And once: 'The thing about good people is they are so – ' long pause, then, 'well, *good*.' With anyone else it would have seemed dotty. But from Joyce she could not have made herself clearer. Sometimes she said, or wrote, in a letter: 'It is perfectly true. God *is* love.'

I had no idea Joyce was a Christian Scientist until she had visited me nearly every day in hospital for several weeks, taken down my shopping list, done my shopping, and, when she and Reggie did not take the children back to the flat for tea, taken a stew or salad round to them by taxi, and, while she was there, emptied our dustbins. She never came to the hospital at visiting times, but slipped in with ward sister's approval almost unnoticed. Once I was howling my head off in supposed privacy when Joyce's beaming face appeared round the cubicle curtains. 'What's the matter? Are you expected to die or something?' she said cheerfully. 'Or are you like the old man I met on the stairs who said he hadn't *been* for a fortnight?' Tears turned, as they say, to instant giggles – in fact, due to an unnecessarily alarming diagnosis, I *was* expecting to die. But Joyce could not see that it mattered one way or another. 'I expect there are lots of forms of death until we really do recognise our total spirituality,' she supposed, not without sympathy, but what mattered at this moment was that the tank in the attic had frozen up, like a lot of other people's, and despite endless attempts she could not get a plumber before the children's normal bath-time; though she supposed from the children's point of view it was a positive benefaction. Had I heard the seasonable misquote 'Bubble bubble, toilet trouble?' As for death, well, it was just like any other horizon, depending where you saw it from.

When she left I felt on top of the world. So did my fellow patients, who had not even talked to her. They wanted to know why, when Joyce came into the ward, however much their aches and pains hurt, they felt cheered up and able to bear them. It was not as though she sang or danced or did any of her funny voices. We just all felt *safe*. I asked her next day why. 'It's not me,' she said in a matter of fact way. 'It's God.' When she told me about Christian Science I was amazed. I had always thought Christian Scientists had no truck with illness, medicine and hospitals, and yet here was Joyce apparently taking the greatest practical interest, just like an ordinary person, in the three or four exploratory operations I had. I asked for Christian Science literature, and she brought it and took out a subscription for me for years for the *Christian Science Monitor*, part of which the entire family read avidly, particularly the arts page, wild life and a marvellous potted edition of the political situation of the entire world every week.

I wanted to write about this, and Joyce said, 'Yes do, darling. But for heaven's sake don't say it's me.'

'Why not? Are you shy?'

'Could be.'

'Well, who shall I say told me all this?'

'Call me Kate. I think I'll be a journalist. I was once you know.

And Reggie can be Tom. Look, I think I'll write in the holy bits myself.' And she did. It's all in a book, written by me except for Joyce's pithy little bits, called *Scrambled Egg for Christmas*.

There is no doubt that I owe the subsequent much better health than I had ever had before to Joyce's introduction to Christian Science, although I realised my attachment to the Church of England, in which I had been brought up as a parson's daughter, was too strong to leave it for Christian Science – not that Joyce ever suggested that I should. What talks we had about it! Each could feed the other. My mother's forebears were Quakers, so there was a certain amount of the 'direct access' that Joyce loved between heart and heaven that was already picked up at my own mother's knee. I have only lately noticed how much Joyce had in common, in her own interpretation of Christian Science, with the best of the truly good unbigoted early Quakers – of there being something of God's spirit in us all, of their unwavering faith, the simplicity and purity of their dress and speech and food.

Long before I knew about Joyce's faith, she asked me to lunch with her in New York, and she chose a very grand uptown restaurant, then ordered poached eggs on toast. I did not know her well enough in those days not to agree to join her in innocent fare, which was what I was mostly living on, made on a gas ring in my bed-sit, and so could have done with a lamb chop. I am glad now I did agree because it proved that good times do not necessarily depend upon rich dishes.

'Don't look now,' Joyce said out of the side of her mouth, 'but the second on the right behind the feathers, don't you *adore* the two bunches of violets clapped over the lug-holes?' She talked to the waiter in a Deep South accent and to a cockney-speaking French fan in his own idiom; both were, of course, enchanted. Then she took me home to her brother's apartment to meet his beautiful ex-model wife and two children, and to talk Kensington Gardens to their English nanny. I had not even mentioned the homesickness that immediately flew out of the window.

When I got to know Joyce better and fussed over *her* getting tired by biting off more than anyone else could chew, and then chewing it, she just hissed back at me: 'Yesss,' pause, and emphatically enunciated: '*Mother.*'

Perhaps I was the mother that she never was, not that she minded, she told me, except at the time when all her contemporaries were having babies and then taking them to their first dancing classes. It was the thing to do, and in a great many ways Joyce liked to conform. Later on she was glad. She was sure she would have been too exacting and bossed her daughters about too much. 'The boot is usually on the other pedal extremity with daughters,' I reminded her. 'They're the ones who do the bossing.'

One of mine had lately been putting me in my place over accepting an invitation to hold her sister's wedding reception in an unmarried gentleman's spacious establishment. There was a lot of talk about what people would think, and would we receive the guests side by side? Joyce was not the least bit worried about this particular convention, but she was greatly intrigued by the spark of what she called 'mature romance' that she detected in the situation.

Paul was taken along to be vetted by Joyce and Reggie, and they found masses of old friends in common. Some of my friends cautioned me against the risks of involvement with a man unused to an ever-increasing hoard of young, for Marian and Rachel were already married with babies. But not so Joyce. She egged us both on, assuring me as we were rounding Hyde Park Corner together that Paul couldn't possibly mind Alex planning to become an anarchist when she left school. 'In fact, he might even enjoy swerving her off it,' she said, 'only we don't want the Dutch-looking gentleman with the rolled tent just in front of us swerved off his bike. And I'll tell you another thing about Paul. Don't you love the way he greets every little wonder of nature that he sees and hears as though it's a miracle? Haven't you noticed? Or are you too blinded by Cupid's darts?'

Anyone who has been driven by Joyce will know that, far

from inhibiting confidences, it seemed only to stimulate them. Not that she allowed the course of a discussion in any way to impair her road sense, which was ever acute. She predicted the appearance of vans emerging from side streets several turnings before reaching them, and insisted on getting into lane before any other traffic had begun to think about forming anything so organised. Having established a place in this would-be lane, she would see the sudden possibility of being able to pass a laundry van and then 'get back into lane' the other side of it, before some unsuspecting taxi had an inkling of what had usurped its place. Joyce was a far-sighted, fast-thinking driver, full of knowledgeable little short-cuts round back streets and through unlikely looking mews, barely known by even the most veteran taxi drivers.

In order to get from one place to another quickly and safely with as great an exchange of confidences as possible, there was no need for Joyce actually to sit at the wheel or even, in my experience, to touch it, though the sensation was that she had direct control over it.

'Just ease gently round this Dear Thing on a motor scooter. I think he's worrying about his spots. He doesn't know yet that he's going to have to overtake that milk float, but he'll have to, if he's not going to ride slap into the number 9 bus when it pulls into the Request Stop where that quaint little Old Party's already waving her umbrella. And then, darling, there's the children to think of. They quite obviously adore Paul, just as much as – well – as *anyone* and he's so good. Turn left any minute now and then sharp right and straight under a low-lying archway with a very steep little incline down into some mews. Well, really not much more than a Single Mew, it's so small. Oh, I do so adore good. Good and love and God are all the same really. Quick! Nip in where that taxi's johnny-head-in-airing along. It won't mind. It isn't going anywhere in particular. Good girl! I think it rather liked it. It seemed to jerk it into a sense of purpose.'

Amazingly traffic *did* seem to like Joyce's driving, and often opened up as willingly as the Red Sea for her. Sometimes, when another driver had been particularly accommodating, Joyce would lean out of the window and beam or call out her thanks. Busdrivers particularly appreciated this courtesy and leant down from their cabs as we swept by to call back some matey good cheer.

'We're doing fine,' Joyce would say. 'In fact I think we'll be there rather *too* soon if anything, but I love being early, don't you? It's so restful. If you draw out just a leetle teeny bit, yes, and now – quick – nip in there. Have you thought what you'll say when he pops the question, darling? There, round we go and back into lane. I always find being in lane so cosy, don't you?' Brompton Road, Kensington Gore, Lovers' Lane. All lanes were covered by Joyce's all-embracing affection for them.

Paul and I actually became engaged during a concert at The Maltings, Snape, after a particularly enjoyable dinner with Joyce and Reggie. We were not all sitting together, but at least we were all under one roof, albeit a high one. Paul took me off to celebrate with champagne drunk from pint mugs, so it was not till breakfast-time next morning, the usual time for telephone calls to Joyce, that I broke the news. She and Reggie were as over-joyed as if we had been teenagers, as Joyce herself had been when she married and Janie and Alex were when they married. At Janie's wedding and her reception in my new fiancé's establish-ment, Joyce and Reggie took literally hundreds of photographs.

For our wedding, ten days later, in London, Joyce, as my 'bridesmaid', laced me into a white *crêpe de Chine* dress of hers discreetly dotted with pale green. She laced me in, because this time the buttons failed to meet their holes in front. Joyce re-moved the narrow belt, cut the buttons off with nail scissors leaving holes opposite the official button holes and threaded the belt through them like a shoelace which she covered neatly with a matching scarf. With John Betjeman as Paul's best man, and Eddie giving me away, we all pranced into St Bartholomew the Great, followed by Reggie and the others. A year later we were all back again at the same church for Alex's wedding.

Last week it was Westminster Abbey with hundreds and thousands of others. We all sang fit to bust, Reggie too.

Reggie's sister died three weeks after Joyce, my sister five weeks before. Joyce's last letter to me covered all three. 'Lovely for her to go so swiftly, but a bit tough on the rest of you ... but life *is* continuity. And the going on is the point. I love the feeling that we can never be out of the range of love/God,' and on she goes about books and music ... 'Must go and get some cold ham. Ginny's coming to lunch.'

Two weeks later she was sitting, more glamorous than I can ever before remember seeing her, at Ginny's party to celebrate Joyce and Reggie's forthcoming Golden Wedding anniversary. She greeted all her dearest friends with her usual grace. When she was asked to go over to the piano to sing, she said in her best let's-all-share-in-this together public voice, 'No, thank you. I don't think this is either the time or the place.' If ever there was a time and a place, surely this was it? I was going to ask again: 'Why not? Are you shy?' when I heard her say out of the corner of her mouth to Janie, who was close to her: 'Cor my back aint 'alf giving me the jip.' And next day, on the telephone: 'Oh, yes, flat on my back. But isn't it marvellous? Reggie's learnt to cook. And wasn't it a wonderful party? Everybody was *so happy*.'

Everybody so happy! That's Joyce, and always will be.

JANIE HAMPTON
AND RACHEL ANDERSON
A Fairy Godmother

JANIE: During the freezing winter of 1962 Joyce was a Fairy Godmother to my family. Our widowed mother was in hospital, and my brother and three sisters were either at school or college. I was at primary school. Joyce would arrive unexpectedly at our house, put on her pinny and take over with the housework. Whatever the occasion, she always seemed to be wearing a Chanel suit and a cream silk blouse tied with a large bow. Her skin was very soft and smelt deliciously clean and powdery when she kissed me. I was fascinated by her hair – short and curly on top, and in a tight knot at the back. She once told me that when it was loose she could sit on it. I longed for a crucial pin to fall out so that I could see it tumbling down her back. She sang a lot as she went through the house.

RACHEL: The other children and I spent a lot of time concentrating on worrying about no money, no food, frozen-up water-pipes, the erratic electricity supply, and chiefly our mum being in a hospital so far away. Joyce dropped in, one freezing afternoon, like an unexpected angel with a ready-cooked shepherd's pie in an insulated bag. Unlike most people in London that winter, she didn't say, 'Isn't the weather awful? Aren't the roads terrible? When will it end? Your poor mother looks worse.'

Joyce was on her way to a theatre, was looking very glamorous, and had a car waiting for her outside in the street. But she popped on a pair of pink rubber gloves and gave our kitchen bin a quick wipe-out. 'You'll find, Rachel, that a little drop of Jeyes, every day, keeps it nice.'

For our next supper, Joyce brought Hungarian goulash with red pickled cabbage. We were all huddled miserably round a two-bar fire which wavered on and off because of the overloaded national grid.

'Nice and warm in here, isn't it?' said Joyce brightly, and suggested that we didn't really need both bars on. 'Now you've got up a good fug, one bar's quite enough, wouldn't you say?'

With a flick of her finger, Joyce managed to point out, without actually saying so, that we weren't homeless, frozen or dying (at least, only one of us was), but were a quite healthy, happy family, with nothing to moan about.

When our mother, in hospital, needed cheering up more than we did, Joyce would leave our supper waiting for us in the snow on the step, with a note explaining what it was and how it should be reheated.

JANIE: Just before Christmas my mother gave Joyce a shopping list of presents for all of us and what little money she had. I terribly wanted a party dress that I had seen in Dickins & Jones, but I knew it was far too expensive, and there was no one to make me one.

Hanging beside my stocking on Christmas morning was the prettiest dress I had ever had. It was navy blue organza, trimmed with red velvet bows and white lace – the sort of dress every ten-year-old dreams about. Just as my mother always cut out the C & A labels from our clothes and put them in Harrods boxes, Joyce had cut out the Harvey Nichols label and thrown away the box to disguise its origin.

That year, our stockings were the best ever – presents that were stockingish, but also useful and lasted: a real manicure set, not a toy one, a reversible red leather 'Alice' band, nut-crackers to go with the nuts, a leatherbound diary and a fountain pen that didn't splodge.

After church, and visiting our mother in hospital, we all went to Joyce and Reggie's flat. It is in an anonymous-looking street, but once inside on the top floor there is a friendly mixture of elegance and comfort. Even as a child I never felt intimidated by the pale furnishings and delicately arranged ornaments. I particularly loved the round table that was always covered in tiny pots of fresh flowers. Although they had no children there was a 'family' atmosphere.

There was always a good assortment of people at their flat. They seemed that vague age that isn't married but isn't young either. Perhaps they were really only in their twenties. Joyce would jolly everyone along with silly party games, while Reggie beamed quietly, administering encouragement and prizes. Joyce never took over with the entertainment – she expected everyone to do their bit. One man stood on his head on the *petit-point* butterfly carpet. Eddie and Alex sang carols while I scraped something approaching a tune on my cello.

After a mammoth tea with all the trimmings we opened our 'official' presents from the Grenfells. All the others had been ostensibly from Mama and Father Christmas, even though they were heavily subsidised. All the grown-ups received well-chosen but slightly frivolous presents. Ours were 'sensible' – thick woolly cardigans from Marks & Sparks. I was a little disappointed with the effect over my light frothy new dress.

Once my mother was better, Joyce continued to wave her magic wand over us. When we needed a car to visit our Granny in Sussex at weekends, a blue Ford Anglia arrived like the pumpkin stage-coach at the front door. We were not supposed to know where it had come from; but we had strong suspicions.

Every few months Joyce would ask my mother to bring one of us as a bearer to collect things she and Reggie had finished with. There were unusual-shaped plates and magazines and books, and once two whole bookcases to put them in that they had had when they were first married. And there were pincushions and hat-pins and things Joyce had had to buy at bazaars. Most of all there were all the 'nearly new' clothes. We were given the run of her blouses and anything that there was no hope of my mother squeezing into. During the mini-skirt era I converted many of her silk garments into daring and fairly indecent dresses.

RACHEL: Sorting through a box of Joyce's clothes was like Christmas. She always passed on not just suits and dresses, but shawls and shoes and useful lengths of material for making things, and lots of dramatic dressing-gowns. It was not until just before I married, and Joyce was hurriedly hemming up bridesmaids' dresses for my little sisters and cousins, that it was decided that I ought to have first pick. I chose a bright pink velvet kaftan, with gold and silver embroidered ribbon down the front, and a New York label. As I've never been very tall I had to cut some of the bottom off, but it still looked terrific. I wore it on my honeymoon and after three confinements.

It was so persistently a 'Joyce' garment that whenever I wore it I had the faint sense of her being there too. Just after I had had my first baby, Hannah, one of the nurses, seeing me sitting up in bed in pink velvet with gold ribbon, said, 'What do *you* do for a job? Are you a sort of pop star or something?'

I would have said 'Yes', but something about Joyce's influence stopped me.

When it finally wore out, I passed it on to a playgroup where little boys who want to be princes wear it.

JANIE: Occasionally voluminous stage costumes would arrive escorting the piles of *Punch*, the *New Yorker* and the *Listener* that Joyce and Reggie always passed on. Once, after we had moved to Norfolk and needed upholstery fabrics, Joyce sent us two Victor Stiebel silk taffeta gowns, one magenta pink and the other lime green. They had boned tops and yards of skirts, plus stiff petticoats. Alex and I put them on, stuffing the fronts with socks. We played 'Duchesses' and then climbed a laburnum tree in full flower, marvelling at the ghastly clashing of the colours. The next day they were cut up into two chair-covers and a small pair of curtains (which they still are).

'I don't quite know what Victor would say to this,' Joyce said when she saw them. 'But I can guess.'

As I am a keen dressmaker Joyce sent me wonderful boxes of 'assortments' – the scraps from her tailor-made dresses, lengths of satin ribbon, lace and braid, odd linen napkins and painted doilies, strange and unusual things that still come in handy. When I made her Christmas presents I tried to recycle her own bits back again. One year it was a picture appliqué cushion made entirely of bits of her old clothes. Her thank-you letters made one feel that the gift really was 'just what she wanted'. There was always a little homily at the end about goodness or love, put in a friendly and unpatronising way. They were never typed, only written in her own spidery hand.

When I was a teenager we would have discussions about God and Life that made me think I was having great and profound ideas. Only afterwards did I realise that Joyce had done most of the talking and certainly all the reasoned and deep thinking.

CLIVE JAMES
Out into the Light

It was the chocolate wrappers that made Joyce an overnight sensation as far as Australia was concerned. She was already famous before she arrived, of course. Even in the late 1950s Sydney wasn't *that* far away from England. We had all seen her in the films. But most of her film roles up until that time had been horse-faced Good Old Girls of the Miss Gossage type, so nobody was ready for the elegant, self-possessed creature she turned out to be when she arrived on her first theatrical tour.

The audiences were delighted with her. So, by and large, was she with them, but she didn't like the chocolate wrappers. It was the custom for everyone in the audience to buy a five-shilling box of Winning Post chocolates during the interval and consume the entire contents during the second half. Each chocolate was wrapped individually in crinkly brown paper and there was a printed guide, also on crinkly paper, to help you identify the flavour of each chocolate by its shape. The printed guide made, if anything, even more noise than the wrappings. When the lights went down for the second half the whole audience pulled the lids off their boxes of chocolates – the lids came off with an audible sob, betokening the tightness of the air seal – and started searching through the crinkly wrappers for the chocolate of their choice. It sounded like a million locusts camping on your television aerial.

Joyce put up with it for two nights and then decided it was time to call a halt. On the third night the lights went down, the curtain went up, and they were at it. Instead of launching into her second half opening song, Joyce advanced regally to the footlights and told the audience that if the eating of the chocolates could be delayed until the end of the performance it might be possible to enjoy both her and them, but if the chocolates had to be eaten now then she would be obliged to withdraw. The audience sat stunned, a freshly unwrapped heart-shaped strawberry cream halfway between lap and gaping mouth. There was a long, tense silence. Then from here, there and eventually everywhere came the reluctant sigh of lids being squeezed back on.

The press next day tried to make a thing out of Joyce's queenly intransigence, but the public loved her for it. She would have been a huge success anyway, but after the affair of the chocolates she was something more – an institution. Lyrical wit and perfect aplomb made a heady compound. She would have been impressive enough as a gifted comedienne, but as a gifted comedienne who was also *toujours la grande dame* she was dynamite. At Sydney University we in the Journalists' Club took the bold step of inviting her to lunch. We were frightened stiff that she might say yes, but felt reasonably confident that she would be too busy for anything so unimportant. She double-crossed us by accepting.

On the appointed day we were all on our best behaviour. Drawn up in the carefully prepared University Union dining-room, we must have looked like a firing squad in mufti. She relaxed us by pretending not to notice. Everybody at the table either forgot his manners or else had never had any, but we coped by picking up the same cutlery as she did. Gradually it became apparent that she was prepared to hear something more adventurous than mere pleasantries. We tried to impress her with our knowledge of contemporary humorists – Peter Sellers, Nichols and May, Mort Sahl. She was very good at not damping the conversation by telling us that she knew them all personally, although when the subject switched to Ealing comedies – all of which we knew line by line and frame by frame – she casually let drop some inside knowledge about the geography of Ealing. Think of it: this woman had been to Ealing!

We made attempts to shock her. There was a good deal of swearing, as if to prove that young Australian males with intellectual proclivities were nevertheless tough, dinkum types underneath. By this time dessert had arrived. Joyce chose a pear, decapitated it, and rotated her spoon inside it, extracting the contents undamaged, whereupon the empty skin fell contentedly inwards. It was all done with such inexpressibly accomplished ease that it produced the same effect as the exhortation about the chocolate wrappers. While we sat with mouths ajar, she whipped an Instamatic out of her reticule and photographed us.

Greatly daring, several of us asked if we could write to her. She said we certainly could. My own first letter, rewritten a dozen times, was a model of lapidary prose that made Walter Pater sound like Jack Kerouac. I was staggered when she answered it, saying how much she had enjoyed meeting us all and waxing enthusiastic about the opportunities Australia offered to the committed bird-watcher. I wrote her another letter, perhaps a touch less strained. By now she was back in England, but she answered that one too. In the next letter I enclosed my latest poem, and in her next answer she did me the honour of criticising it in specific and useful detail. This was a particularly selfless gesture, since she must have spotted that I had composed it for the occasion out of no other impulse except the desire to impress. Without letting me know what she was up to, she was once again embarked on her usual task of helping someone to become himself.

I was unpromising material, but perhaps that was the challenge. Much later I realised that there were scores of us whose spiritual welfare she was quietly supervising, but she had the knack of making you feel that you were the only one. We were all her only sons. When I arrived in London, broke to the wide, and absurdly proud of it, she was more patient with my pretensions to radicalism than the occasion warranted. (So was Reg, for that matter, who in my case must have been wondering how much boredom his wife's kindness to waifs and strays was going to let him in for.) At the time I was incapable of realising that my own convictions were essentially a pose and that she was the true radical, since the values she represented were beyond the power of any government either to create or to destroy. But she never mocked me, although once or twice I caught her smiling in the middle of my most moving prepared speech. I was still asked to the Christmas party, where I had to play uncle to several enchanting children she was looking after over the festive season. Joyce describes the scene in her book *In Pleasant Places* but charitably makes no reference to my lurching self-consciousness. It still bothers me that I had neglected to clean my finger-nails.

Artistically creative people often excuse themselves from everyday obligations. But Joyce, who was artistically creative to a high degree, never did, not even once. She was very good at planning her day. Not that she ever let you know how much effort she put into fitting everything in. It all just happened. Once at Elm Park Gardens I spent an hour in hysterics while she tried out some new sketches on me – a privileged audience of one. For me it was the highlight of an idle day, or more probably an idle year. Later on I realised that she must have written a dozen letters that day, seen a dozen people, planned a dozen other days like it. Her use of time was like a classical Latin sentence – packed with meaning, nothing wasted.

As the Feldmarschallin points out to Octavian in *Der Rosenkavalier*, it isn't the what, it's the how. Joyce was an object lesson in how to behave. She never preached, and I am not even sure that she ever set out to teach by example. But it was plain even to an eye as unpractised as mine that her good manners went far below the surface, all the way to the centre of the soul. Her good manners were *good* manners. It gradually occurred to me that doing the right thing meant more than just conforming to some abstract code. The implications of this realisation were disturbing. I might have to abandon my vague expectations of the millennium and settle down to doing something about my clear duties in the present. I tried to stave these thoughts off by mentally enrolling Joyce in the exploiting upper class, but since she obviously worked for a living and was a lot better than I was at treating the lower orders like human beings, this belief was hard to sustain. It even began to occur to me that I did not know very much about life.

I am still learning and always too slowly, but like so many of Joyce's friends I owe to her much of what acumen I have come to possess. Katharine Whitehorn once said that you can tell the person who lives for others by the haunted look on the faces of the others, but Joyce wasn't like that. She never imposed herself for a second. She simply lived her life, and the way that she lived it made you wonder how well you were living yours.

In the last ten years I saw less of her than I might have, perhaps through an unacknowledged conviction that if I had her as a conscience I would never develop one of my own. There was also the danger of sunburn from reflected glory. At Cambridge I invited her as a guest of honour to the Footlights annual dinner. She did a variation on her pear routine and gave a speech that left the congregation of apprentice comedians slack-jawed with the sudden, awful awareness of how much class you had to have before you could be as classy as that. A few years later, still in Cambridge, I was married and a baby was on the way – overdue, in fact. Joyce was playing a week at the Arts Theatre before taking her show into London. She arranged for two chairs to be put in the wings for my wife and myself, explaining to my wife where the nearest loo was. 'You practically have to spend your *life* there at this stage of the proceedings, don't you?' It was complicity between mothers. You would never have guessed that this was the one happiness she had never been granted. But it was a small thing beside the happiness she could cause, as I saw and heard all over again when she walked out into the light.

Then months went by without a meeting and the months stretched into years. At the touch of a button I could see her on *Face the Music*. We talked occasionally on the telephone and more occasionally still we exchanged letters, but she knew that I had broken free. My second mother had joined my first mother as someone to grow apart from. Those of us who must learn self-possession, instead of attaining it by instinct, are often jealous of our isolation, and guard it hardest against those who taught us most. Perhaps I am trying to find a good name for ingratitude.

But in the last year of Joyce's life I somehow reached the conclusion that we had better meet soon. She gave me lunch at Elm Park Gardens. As always it seemed no time since the last time. For once doing the right thing at the right moment, I tried to thank her for what she had done for me. Some of what I had to say is in this article, which is the inadequate record of how she helped one young man to find his way. The hundreds of others whose lives were touched by her must all have stories like it. Beyond those favoured hundreds who knew her in person are the thousands and the millions who could tell just from the look of her that she had a unique spirit. There was a day when a woman who aroused as much loving gratitude as that would have been canonised for it. So far Christian Scientists have got along without saints but perhaps in her case they should think again. Meanwhile she remains an unforgettable example of just how extraordinary an ordinary human being can be.

JOYCE GRENFELL

Lunchtime Concert

Grey clergyman of eighty, next to me,
Lover of music though you well may be
Yours was not a Christian way to act
This afternoon, and that, Sir, is a fact.
Crisp wheaten biscuits topped with slabs of cheese
Drawn from a paper bag upon the knees
May make an appetizing sort of lunch;
They also wreck the music, for they crunch.
And having crunched, the drier crumbs break off
And play old Harry with your dear old cough.
Grey clergyman of eighty, next to me,
Lover of Mozart though you seemed to be
I wonder how you heard a single note
What with the crunch, and clearing of your throat.
As Nanny used to say so long ago:
You never did of ought to of, you know.

JOSEPH COOPER
Musical Games

When, in August 1973, my first wife Jean died of cancer Joyce helped to pick up the bits that were left of me and get them into working order – no preaching, no exhortations – but regular telephone calls with some amusing tit-bits, and invitations to join her for picnic lunch, as Reggie was out and she wanted me to try out a new soup, or a new pudding. The soup was good: so was the pudding. But the treatment was miraculous.

It so happened that a mass of invitations to very important functions were coming in, which I told Joyce all about. It wasn't until about five years later that I began to realise that all the crested cards which graced my mantelpiece at that time had been quietly engineered by none other than Joyce herself. She never wanted any credit – in fact the subject would have been changed with lightning speed. As Clive James has said: 'She was one of the few people I've ever met who actually did do good by stealth.'

One of Joyce's greatest assets on *Face the Music* was her natural capacity for being the same person to everybody. The sheer joy of being alive, and revelling in whatever she was doing, infected all those around her. Bernard Levin like the rest of us came under her spell. At their first reunion in Joyce's last series of *Face the Music* I was standing outside my dressing-room door when I saw them joyfully rush into each other's arms for a long, affectionate embrace.

Whether Joyce felt nervous before a *Face the Music* programme it is impossible to say. Her old friend Dame Myra Hess before a concert used to be seen emerging from her dressing-room the picture of gloom and fear, and would only turn on her radiant smile as she walked on to the platform. Joyce, on the other hand, could be heard before a programme chatting and giggling with her team-mates until it was time for them to take their bow and go to their chairs on the set. Joyce would invariably sing a loud arpeggio, in imitation of the operatic star vocalising off stage. This always got a laugh. But Joyce observed the quantity of the laugh and judged from it the kind of audience they were. I believe (though she never discussed the matter in detail) that she did adapt her style to the particular kind of studio audience. If the vocal arpeggio was greeted by a roar of delight Joyce, and specially her two 'boys', tended to respond by off-the-cuff quips and gibes, which occasionally came near to slapstick. Joyce could moderate this by a look at each in turn – almost as if she were saying, 'George, don't do that.' Afterwards Joyce would whisper to me (and not expect an answer), 'I thought they were getting just a bit out of hand, so I quietened them down.'

Many years before *Face the Music* started on B.B.C. Television in 1966, its prototype *Call the Tune* enjoyed a highly successful four-year run on Radio (the old Home Service). Joyce was one of the lady panellists and I was chairman. So, off and on, Joyce and I were quizzing musically for about twenty-five years. Joyce, who had a mania for punctuality, often arrived in the sound studio at Broadcasting House early; one day she said, 'Let's make up a song. You play an introduction to a mock Schumann *Lied*, and I'll enter at a suitable moment.'

The rest is history among the participants of *Call the Tune* and *Face the Music*. We tried Debussy, Handel, English Nymphs and Shepherds, and Russian. The trouble was we couldn't do it to order, and yet we needed enthusiasts to egg us on and get the adrenalin going. Joyce's regular pianist during her stage career, William Blezard, used to do it too. Bill and I are neighbours and friends, and neither of us can explain the sheer genius of Joyce's contribution. Not only was she making up nonsense words with an impeccable German or French accent (I cannot judge her Russian), but she would take a musical suggestion from the pianist, elaborate it and then provide a new section which the pianist would develop. I still have a few tapes which 'caught us in the act' and therefore in rather good form; in one made in 1957 Gerard Hoffnung, a regular panellist, can be heard splitting his sides.

Joyce seemed to contain a constant stream of music in her head, all ready in the right key, waiting for the tap to be turned on. For example, in the television studio I once played the D flat on the piano which starts Debussy's *The Girl with the Flaxen Hair*. Joyce couldn't see the piano from where she was sitting, nor did she know what piece I had in mind. But when I said, 'What comes next?' she instantly continued with the correct notes of the Debussy. At a session months later, I sat in my Question-master's chair, with Joyce in her accustomed seat (i.e. both away from the piano). I said to Joyce, 'Sing the opening note of *The Girl with the Flaxen Hair*': without a second's pause for thought, she sang the first note. I rushed to the piano and found she had sung the D flat in perfect pitch.

Her aural observation extended to the pronunciation of foreign composers. I used to love hearing her say 'Bach' or 'Schumann' – two names which, in particular, trouble some of our most distinguished English musicians, but which slipped off her tongue as a German would say them.

Sometimes Joyce's inner ear and her musical knowledge were in conflict: I was playing Dvořák's *Humoresque* on the dummy keyboard. Joyce said, 'I seem to hear a violin.' She started to hum the Dvořák correctly, but had only previously heard it as a violin Encore and had no idea that it had originally been composed for piano.

During the Hidden Melody (where a familiar tune is buried in the texture of a piece, simulating a certain composer's style, e.g. *Three Blind Mice à la* Debussy) I used to watch the team through the corner of my eye. When Robin Ray and Joyce were on together they often spotted the hidden tune at the same split second; Robin nearly always spotted the composer's style first.

Sometimes Richard Baker would trounce Robin and Joyce by keeping poker-faced until I stopped, and then in a flash trotting out the hidden tune and the composer. But whoever won, it was Joyce who made the game a matter of great moment and excitement.

Although Joyce was a regular concert-goer I think she preferred the peace and intimacy of listening in at home. But she always looked forward to her yearly visits to the Aldeburgh Festival, and liked and got to know well the music of Benjamin Britten. Other composers who specially appealed to her were Elgar, Bach, Vaughan Williams, but most of all Mozart.

Joyce was once sitting in the row in front of me at a charity concert in the Fairfield Hall, Croydon. Clifford Curzon was the soloist in the Mozart Piano Concerto in B flat, K.595. He was in peak form and the whole performance was one of matchless, unearthly beauty. The audience were so immersed that it must have been at least five seconds before they jerked back to reality and started to applaud. Joyce turned in my direction and said, 'Curzon is the one for me. You can keep the rest.'

At Westminster Abbey on 7 February 1980 at the Service of Thanksgiving for the life of Joyce Grenfell, amid the vast throng that filled every corner of the building, Sir Clifford Curzon came – unannounced, with touching humility – to pay his last respects to a great lady of our time.

RICHARD BAKER

A Favourite Aunt

I shared my first impression of Joyce Grenfell with the millions of others who thought her a riot in the St Trinian's films – all toothy grin and jolly hockey sticks. I came a trifle closer, when, as a Third Programme announcer in what must be regarded as the vintage days of the early fifties, I sometimes made the opening announcements for Stephen Potter and Co. in the famous 'How' series and then sat down to suppress my laughter at Joyce's hilarious contributions to those programmes. But I did not actually meet her until, in 1966, I was invited by Walter Todds to appear with her on a new television music quiz called *Face the Music*. On that occasion I remember I approached her with the deference of a devoted fan, and for all the fondness I subsequently developed, I continued to feel I was a privileged member of the admiring throng.

We must have sat together on the panel of *Face the Music* two or three dozen times, more often than not with Robin Ray on the other side of her. I don't think Robin would mind me saying that for all his erudition and ready wit, it was Joyce who dominated our trio. She did so naturally and delightfully, without the least effort and without giving the smallest offence. She was a star.

Although the early editions of *Face the Music* were recorded in London, and we returned to Shepherd's Bush for the last series, most of the programmes were recorded in Manchester, latterly in the B.B.C.'s new studios, but for several years at the old converted chapel in Dickinson Road where conditions were far from ideal but, as so often happens in such circumstances, the atmosphere was warmly perfect. The studio audience was small, probably not more than a hundred or so, and many people came time after time. There was no barrier between us and them, such as inevitably exists on the stage of the Television Theatre, where Joyce recorded her final *Face the Music* appearances, and the old Dickinson Road studio, though we grumbled about it sometimes, was the perfect setting for an intimate entertainment such as ours. Joyce certainly flourished there. She made friends with the audience at once, making them feel not so much spectators as accomplices in what was about to take place.

As for her fellow-panellists, she took us under her wing in the fashion of a mother or favourite aunt and admonished us mock-seriously (or was it seriously?) if we overstepped her own limits of propriety. Since she ate sparingly, drank no alcohol and did not smoke, these limits could seem constricting, especially during the rather long 'hospitality' period between our brief lighting rehearsal and the recording itself. But although restrained to the point of austerity where eating and drinking were concerned, she was always the life and soul of these interludes as of every other party she attended. And when she expressed her disapproval of over-indulgence, it was always done with the utmost good humour, for our own good. Joyce was solicitous for the welfare of her friends and wanted everyone to be as naturally happy as she was.

Although I vaguely knew she was a Christian Scientist, she never pressed her beliefs on others, and it was only gradually that I came to understand how profound and how active her faith was. On one train journey north, I remember we discussed a Cathedral address she was to give, but only since her death have I discovered how ceaselessly and tirelessly she spoke and wrote about the Christian message. Because I gave a short tribute to Joyce in the B.B.C. T.V. nine o'clock news on the night she died, I heard from many people who had corresponded with her over the years, some of them enclosing letters Joyce had written to them. Her letters were lengthy, though they must have been very numerous indeed. In one that lies before me now, she answers what she calls '*the* big question – how a God of Love can permit suffering'.

Joyce argues in this letter that God, who is perfect, does not allow suffering. It happens because we are deceived by the 'counterfeit power of evil'; suffering and sin are no more real and lasting than the human body which dies. All that is imperfect vanishes before 'the only real power, God, who is love'. We can get more and more idea of God's love by 'losing the sense of human limitation, acknowledging that our only true place is in God's mind, inseparable from him'. This process, Joyce admits, is a full-time job 'but the rewards of studying, praying and seeing evidence of God's goodness are in proportion to our desire to learn and experience – the *Be Still and Know* feeling'.

Joyce was happy to speak about spiritual matters to sceptics, and particularly enjoyed dealing with student audiences. She had a ready answer for one young man who asked how he could recognise 'the spiritual'. 'Would you recognise honesty, kindness, humour, selflessness, loyalty and generosity?' asked Joyce. 'Yes,' was the reply. 'Then you have no difficulty,' said Joyce. 'These are all spiritual qualities which we do not recognise with our brain or our five senses. We recognise them with our own spiritual perception which comes to us because we reflect, in our spiritual being, the perfection of God.'

Such were the arguments in favour of her beliefs that Joyce advanced, when asked, on platforms, in pulpits sometimes or in private letters. I know now that she spent part of every day in contemplation and spiritual reading. But at the time when we met frequently on *Face the Music* there was no mention of such things. Her conversation was matter-of-fact and often funny. She would usually have some new anecdote to tell us of a chance encounter in hotel or train, which could, one felt, easily become the germ of yet another character study. I recall her more-in-sorrow-than-in-anger look, for example, as she repeated her butcher's comment when she called into the shop on the day after one of our programmes had gone out on the air. Instead of asking what she wanted, he merely shook his head sadly and said,

'Oh, Mrs Grenfell, fancy you not knowing Puccini's "*Vissi d'Arte*"!' Joyce's observation of fellow human beings was ceaseless and sharp, though never malicious, and she had an inimitable way of sharing a joke. This was only partly a matter of words. Whether her audience was numbered in thousands or consisted of a single friend, she brought into play a formidable armoury of gestures, facial expressions, inflections and perfectly-timed pauses.

Spontaneous, friendly and open though she was, there was inevitably a trace of grandeur about Joyce, and she was not tolerant of the shoddy or second-rate in any aspect of life. Her critical standards as applied to literature, television, films, the theatre, or the passing scene, were extremely exacting though never personally uncharitable, and I well remember her reply when someone suggested we should all stay at a large modern hotel in Manchester. 'Oh no,' said Joyce, 'I always stay at the Midland. They still have linen sheets.'

The high standards Joyce hoped for in others, she relentlessly demanded of herself. This accounts for the polished perfection of her songs and monologues and the excellence of her two volumes of autobiography. To give just one small example of her attention to detail: she wanted a photograph of me to include in the second volume *In Pleasant Places* and was not happy with any that were readily available. She would not be satisfied until we unearthed a pile of family snapshots, one of which she eventually chose because it was 'the Dicky she knew'.

To have Joyce's friendship was a stimulus as well as a comfort, for it was not easy to be worthy of it. At Christmas she would send out charming coloured caricatures of herself. They were not reproduced. Each one was drawn individually, and this fact points to the most important ingredient of her charm. No matter how much trouble was involved, she never allowed success to make her impersonal.

Honesty, kindness, humour, selflessness, loyalty and generosity – those qualities which denote the spirit – Joyce possessed abundantly. She laboured with meticulous devotion in the great cause of cheering us all up, and her cheerfulness went very deep. She believed that life, despite its vexing eccentricities, is essentially good, and made the rest of us think so too. It was a noble achievement.

JOYCE GRENFELL
Opera Interval

Bravo ... Bravo.

(*Applauding*) Oh, how lovely.

Wasn't it heavenly?

Bravo ... Bravo.

Isn't she marvellous? That voice. It really is celestial. And he was *so* good, wasn't he? The one in the middle. The one in blue. You know, the main man. *Lovely* voice.

(*Gets up to let people pass*) Can you manage?

Do you want to go out and mingle a little and see who is here – or shall we stay here and digest what we've just heard? All right – let's digest now and mingle later.

Do you know, I think that when I was very very young I heard Belushkin sing that part, only he sang it lower.

I must confess I got a little confused in the story, did you? I know she's a twin and there was a muddle, but I can't *quite* remember why she starts off in that pretty white dress, and then when she comes in again later she's dressed as a Crusader. It's probably a disguise. But one wonders why?

She's the daughter of the man in black, I suppose. The one who sang at the top of the stairs with that lovely voice. Let's look it up and see who is who.

'Don Penzalo, a wealthy landowner.' (That's probably her father.) 'Mildura ...' that's her I think ... 'daughter to the Duke of Pantilla.' Oh, not Don Penzalo then. No ... 'The Duke of Pantilla, father of Mildura.' Well, there we are.

'Zelda, an old nurse.' Yes, we have seen her. She's the one with two sticks and rather a rumbly voice, remember?

'Fedora, a confidante.'

'Boldoni, a bodyguard.'

'Don Alfredo, a general in the Crusaders.' Ah, Crusaders.

'Chorus of Fisherfolk, Villagers, Haymakers, Courtiers and Crusaders.' We haven't seen the Courtiers and Crusaders yet, but we've seen the fisherfolk, villagers and haymakers – yes, we have. They were the ones with fishing-nets and rakes and things.

You know, one ought to do one's homework before one goes to the opera. I've got a little book that tells you all the stories, but I never can remember to look it up till I get home, then it's too late.

Let's see what we have just seen:

Oh, it was a market place – I thought so.

'Act I. The Market Place of Pola.

'As dawn breaks over the sleepy village of Pola in Pantilla fisherfolk on their way to work join with villagers and hay-makers to express their concern over the Royalist cause.'

Oh ... *that's* what they were doing.

'Mildura pines for her lover, Don Alfredo, who is preparing to leave for the Crusades' ... ah, there you are ... 'and disguises herself in order to join him in Malta.'

Oh, Malta. Dear Malta. How I love it.

Do you know it well?

I used to go there a great deal when I was a gel, and one had such fun. I used to go and stay with darling old Admiral Sir Cardington Dexter and his wife Nadia. Did you know Nadia? She was a *little* strange! He met her in Casablanca! Yes, exactly. But I won't hear a word against her, because she was always very kind to me. Oh, it was such fun in those days. So gay. Parties, parties and more parties. Heavenly young men in uniform – white naval uniform, quite irresistible, and you know, honestly, one hardly noticed the Maltese at all.

Now. 'Mildura disguises herself in order to join Don Alfredo, but Don Penzalo' (I'm sure he's the one in blue) 'seeks revenge for a slight done him by the Duke and plans to abduct Mildura, whom he suspects of political duplicity, and flee with her to Spain.' Oh, Spain. Very *mouvementé*! Do you know Spain well?

No, Italy is my passion. *Bella Italia*. I always feel very hard done by if I don't get my annual ration of *Bella Italia*. It's so nourishing.

'Zelda, an old nurse, reads warnings in the stars and begs Mildura to delay her departure until the harvest is gathered in. Don Penzalo does not recognise Mildura and challenges her to a duet.' That's what it says: 'Challenges her to a du—' Oh, I am idiotic. The light's so bad in here.

(*Gets up to let people pass back to their seats.*)

I'm so sorry. Can you get by? Ow – No, it's all right, only a *tiny* little ladder ...

One really ought to come to the opera more often. I do love it so. My mother used to go a great deal. She loved it, and, of course, she was very musical. Oh, very. She had a most enchanting gift, she played the piano entirely by heart, well I suppose you could call it by ear. She never had a lesson in her life. She would go to an opera, hear it, and then come home and play the entire thing (oh, I'm so sorry, did I hit you?). She'd play the entire thing from memory without a note of music. So, of course, I grew up knowing all the lovely lovely tunes one knows so well. It is such an advantage – one step ahead of everyone else.

No, alas, I don't play.

Are you getting hungry?

It's a very long opera, three more Acts. Are you sure you aren't hungry? I should have fed you better. A boiled egg isn't enough for opera. I do hope you won't wilt.

No, I *love* it. I'm afraid it's all food and drink to me. Oh, there the lights are going down – it's too exciting – I'm like a child at the theatre.

(*Applauds.*) I don't know who the conductor is, but he's supposed to be very well known.

Oh dear, we don't know where we are, do we. Well, we do. We're in the Cloisters of the Cathedral of St Geminiano. Sh. Sh. Sh.

BERNARD LEVIN

A Civilised Woman

For those who had the luck to know Joyce Grenfell, and I dare say for millions who never met her but had seen her performances on the stage, the cinema and television, the image that remains most vividly is of a woman laughing. That, as I close my eyes, is what I see and hear: a moment later, I begin to laugh myself.

Joyce was funny – naturally, gracefully and unstintingly. But that was not the only reason for our laughter. In her we recognised someone who made fun without malice, depicted absurdity with love, left her audiences not only smiling, but deeply happy. She had seized on a profound truth; that it is the foibles and follies of the human race that make it human, and she invited us to laugh at ourselves and at others because she understood that it truly is one touch of laughter that makes the whole world kin.

Only those who knew her off-stage also knew that she was a very serious woman, too, and that her seriousness was rooted in a deep religious faith. She was a Christian Scientist, and wonderfully secure in her beliefs. But you had to know her to know that, because it was something inner and private; she did not hide it, but neither did she go about brandishing it.

Her faith, her work, her marriage; these were the three columns that held her life so serene and secure. She once confided to me over dinner after a performance of *Face the Music* that that day was her wedding anniversary, and as I opened my mouth to communicate the news to the rest of the table, so that we could at least drink to her and Reggie, she hushed me vigorously; that, too, was something private. But I shall not forget the note of love and pride in her voice as she added reflectively, 'Yes, I've been married for forty years, to the same nice man.'

For all that time and more she was the same nice woman. And she was something else, something that constituted one of the most important of her qualities. She was English, in a sense far wider and more important than the details on her birth certificate. She embodied certain qualities of tolerance (she had strong political views, also never revealed in public), kindness, robustness, charm and optimism that do represent something essentially and vitally English, and I know that she deeply regretted, though she never wasted time in vain nostalgia, the inexorable decline in such qualities over the past two or three decades. Joyce was a civilised woman; I use the word as the highest term of praise in my vocabulary, meaning one whose *douceur de vivre* was a positive thing, offered as freely to others as it was enjoyed by her.

At sixty-nine, she had time to write and publish two volumes of autobiography; *finis coronat opus*, for you can hear her voice, and take the measure of her mind and character, on every page of *Joyce Grenfell Requests the Pleasure* and *In Pleasant Places*. As a very well-read woman she would have made a face at anyone who did not know where the second title came from. I know she will forgive me when I confess that I have just had to look it up, but I am glad I did, for I cannot think of a more fitting epitaph for my dear, good, laughing friend: 'The lines are fallen unto me in pleasant places; yea, I have a goodly heritage.'

JOHN DANKWORTH
AND CLEO LAINE

Music Without Barriers

JOHN: Joyce and Reggie's visits to our household involved every type of occasion from the Royal to the very humble. They came about as a result of much earlier happenings.

CLEO: Joyce came into my life, long before we ever met, when I first heard the record of her singing the song that she wrote with Richard Addinsell, 'I'm Going to See You Today'. It was long before I took up professional singing – I was a late starter just as she was – but I used to try to imitate her enchanting version of that song. I never got it quite right.

JOHN: Our meeting with the Grenfells took place when Joyce, Cleo, Ben Luxon and Richard Rodney Bennett got together for an entertainment based on the music of Noël Coward. It was staged at the Aldeburgh Festival in 1970, directed by Colin Graham. Cleo and Joyce seemed to hit it off immediately despite a certain disparity of age and backgrounds.

CLEO: We seemed to fall about like a couple of schoolgirls at the slightest provocation. At one rehearsal of the Coward show Joyce, Ben, Richard and I had to sing the intricate lyrics of 'Mad Dogs and Englishmen'. When it came to the 'doo-wacka-doo' chorus bit a purely accidental slip of the tongue from Joyce made the phrase sound nonsensical and perhaps a little *risqué*. The four of us collapsed into helpless laughter, the sort of rib-aching hysteria that sounds boring when you try to explain, but everyone knows what I mean. Colin, sitting in the dark of the theatre, got very cross with us when it went on too long. Like a schoolteacher he boomed from the stalls, 'Very well, get it out of your systems. And then we can go on.' And like naughty school-kids we resumed, still struggling to control our explosions. I won't ever forget that incident.

JOHN: We kept in touch with Joyce and Reggie after that – and they with us. Joyce sent her unique little notelets, and we usually managed to dispatch a postcard to Elm Park Gardens from whichever exotic or tawdry corner of the world we happened to be in at the time.

When we started the Wavendon All-Music Plan in 1969 – a music trust centred round a small concert hall in our back garden – Joyce was one of the first of our entertainer friends to rally to our aid. Our mission at Wavendon was – and still is – to attempt to break down the barriers between 'art music' and popular music, and it proved to be a cause near and dear to Joyce's heart. Perhaps it was because in our policy of juxtaposing many different facets of the great world of music she saw a re-flection of her own successful experiments in rapidly changing moods and 'depths' as a performer.

She came to our aid many times to raise funds, to perform or to encourage us when our hearts were getting faint.

CLEO: She was obviously a pastmaster at charity money-raising events, and our comparative naïveté sometimes appalled her. Once we irritated her so much that her 'bossy, taking-over' side came to the fore.

We had a fête in our garden, which in addition to a Celebrity Corner boasted side-shows, bring-and-buy stalls and a tent where cast-offs from my wardrobe – known for the occasion as 'Cleo's Clobber' – were sold at marked-down prices. Joyce announced her arrival that morning with her usual 'Cooee – anyone at home?' in our hallway. I responded, coming down-stairs with a large armful of clothes, priced for the 'Clobber' tent.

Joyce looked at the price on one of my dresses – and took over straight away. 'You can't sell it at that price, my dear, much too cheap – come along, let's get this done right.' She whisked both clothes and me over to the tent, got the prices altered, and proceeded to sell them with the ease and expertise of a Petticoat Lane stallholder, coercing people into parting with amazing amounts of money. And she wouldn't even sign an autograph unless it was paid for.

We made more money from 'Cleo's Clobber' than from any of the other stalls. From that day on I never minded Joyce being a 'bossy-boots'. It was generally for a good reason, and on this occasion for a good cause.

JOHN : Others in this book will have no doubt discussed Joyce's religion and her deep convictions on life. I suppose Cleo and I have similar philosophies, although they are not channelled into one particular theological or humanist argument. But Joyce's behaviour never supported the thought that a devout person should not be able to laugh at less than devout things. She was no saint, and occasionally her impish sense of humour was, I believe, designed to have an unsettling effect, or at least to test the nerves of those present.

One such occasion was in the summer of 1979, when I was standing chatting alone to a 'royal personage' before a concert in which Joyce was involved. No one else was within earshot. Joyce joined us and was obviously bursting to tell us the latest story in her repertoire. It was a distinctly rude story about two nuns and a crossword-puzzle. I had anxious moments while Joyce told that story, but neither of us was offended by it. If ever any doubt had existed in my mind – and I must admit that very occasionally it had – I found out that night for certain that Joyce was emphatically not a prude.

CLEO : Her love of music was common knowledge as a result of her T.V. appearances, but the wideness of her musical tastes was not so generally known. Neither was the quality of her own singing voice, which was natural and unpretentious. She didn't reckon it much, so she was amazed – and I think a little flattered – when I told her how good I thought it was. She was always worried about singing out of tune, and during our rehearsals for the Noël Coward programme she would ask constantly if she was on pitch. Richard and I would always reassure her, but I think she was convinced we were being kind. We weren't – one of the reasons I fell for her voice before we met was her 'in-tuneness'. Joyce denigrated her own singing, and it was the same with her musical knowledge. But again, during those rehearsals, Richard and I soon found out that it was not only classical music that she knew – and had strong views about. It was the same with popular music, jazz and 'show' songs. Often she would play on the piano something from the music-hall era, dragging words from an apparently unlimited bank of lyrics tucked somewhere in her head. Such odd ditties would crease us all up again when we'd become too intense through working hard.

I think pretentious music of any kind was her real hate. And she didn't mince her words if she thought a performer was putting on airs and graces. I valued her opinion highly, and often asked her what she felt about an interpretation. She was always honest, telling me if I was overdoing it or otherwise. Often on record programmes of her own choice she would slip in a record of mine, usually 'On a Clear Day' – one of her favourites – or one of the poetry settings. She loved John's music too, and thought our group superb. But she did think our pianist Paul Hart could do with a haircut!

JOHN: When we extended our auditorium at Wavendon Joyce agreed to be part of the opening-night celebrations in the summer of 1979. But she made us promise that she would not be expected to do her 'show' – she had some time ago announced her retirement from that, and indeed had bequeathed her beloved 'throat microphone' to our stage property-box. She said her contribution would be an 'informal talk'.

We took tremendous trouble to explain the distinction to our audience that night. But, honestly, we need not have bothered. From the moment she stepped into the stage lighting Joyce became an entertainer, and our audience – not by any means an uncritical one – her slaves. Although the 'produced' part of her show was missing (and her enchanting musical offerings too) the basic element of a Grenfell appearance – timing – was as expertly dispensed as it had ever been, and her 'non-show' was one of the most skilfully-woven tapestries of verbal light and shade one could ever hope to witness. To observe that it was, to my knowledge, the last-but-one performance that Joyce gave suggests a morbid pride in something one should be anything but happy about, but nevertheless I'm so glad that Cleo and I were there.

RICHARD HOGGART

The Noblest Roman of Them All

Joyce Grenfell and the Pilkington Committee

Someone, somewhere, once told me about an essay on what might be called 'the psycho-sociology of national committees'. The theory it propounded appeared to fit exactly one main characteristic of the Pilkington Committee on Broadcasting. That committee, a mixed bag of eleven people, sat from 1960 to 1962 under the chairmanship of Sir Harry, now Lord, Pilkington. I've never been able to find the above essay and the eminent academic person to whom I tried to ascribe it politely denied paternity. The part of it which most intrigued me argued that national committees on complex matters of public concern, traditionally composed almost wholly of 'intelligent laymen and laywomen' (that is, not specialists or people with a pronounced prior public stance on the matter under review), tend to set up within their own corporate bodies, by a sort of instinct, a Gladiators-and-Romans pattern.

So most members of such a committee come to its work fresh, ignorant and uncommitted but, or this is the assumption, anxious to be fair and objective. They have to sort out and digest a great mass of oral and written material, much of it factual, much also seeking to be persuasive, though running in all directions. These, the majority, are the Romans of such a conventionally-composed committee.

A few other members, either because they already know a good deal about the subject, or because they are naturally combative and quick on their feet, or through a combination of all these, move as it were to the front of the stage and between them slog out the main issues, not only for themselves but for the benefit of the others. They dramatise and sharpen the main arguments. These are the Gladiators.

The Gladiators no doubt seem dashing, the front runners; and to some extent they are. But in the end they have only as much power as is contained in their capacity to persuade and convince the Romans; and the Romans, though they may not be specialists, do tend to be shrewd and not easily bowled over.

Joyce Grenfell was very pleased and proud to be invited to serve on Pilkington (so were most of us, I think). But she felt herself less well-equipped than most others; after all, she hadn't been to university; she hadn't had political experience; she was a public entertainer but a very private person. She needn't have worried. There were some very good members of the Committee. The other woman, Betty Whitley of Edinburgh, for example, was also a formidable listener, questioner and reflector on what she'd heard and read. She had already had much public experience, so knew her way around. So it's no disrespect to her contribution – indeed, I am sure she would agree with me – to say that Joyce was the most splendid Roman of us all, since she started virtually from scratch in this strange set of rituals.

If you convinced Joyce Grenfell about a point of view, you knew you had come through a very fine mill indeed. You also soon learned that once convinced she stayed firm; flattery from someone of a different persuasion or talk of the needs of expediency, for compromise, would not move her. She became the litmus paper, the geiger-counter, the bench-mark of the sound sense and honesty of the Committee's thinking. That, when the Report appeared, some people did not see how good a piece of work it was but greeted it with howls of rage – often because their own greed in misusing a public facility had been exposed – moved her not at all, either at the time of publication or in the years after. She remained extremely proud of having served, and more than anyone of us kept alive – by her cards and messages of one sort or another in the two decades thereafter – something of our group sense, that of people who had gone through a great deal together.

I felt that this was, for me at least, the right way to begin these memories of Joyce, since such an approach brings out, above all, her exceptional directness. She was not an intellectual in the usual sense; nor did she regard herself as one. She had an enquiring but not a speculative mind, and her unshakeable Christian faith emerged naturally from that kind of spirit. She was full of uncommon common sense, persistent, frank and probing. During the progress of Pilkington we gradually became more than committee acquaintances; we became friends, and the friendship very soon broadened to include Reggie and my own wife. Like all good friendships, ours was based on some admiration for qualities in one another, plus regret that blind spots existed and persisted. As to such areas, though she did not nag, Joyce could not forbear from trying to make an improvement. This pertinacity ensured that she could not easily or for long settle with what she regarded as my own chief blind spot – my views on 'class', its persistence and its effects. She just didn't believe that class feeling and class differences mattered much any more; she felt she'd got rid of them herself, so why couldn't I?

The other great quality which she brought to the Pilkington Committee's deliberations was gaiety. I don't think she was capable of malice: she did not greatly care for gossip and her jokes were therefore not unkind towards others. What she displayed could more accurately be described as a sense of fun nourished by affectionate observation of our idiosyncrasies. As the giving of oral evidence rolled on day by day (and we met frequently) she would, whilst listening closely, sketch her colleagues or those giving evidence. The results were a cross between pencil portraits and caricatures, but nearer the first.

She was capable of practising and enjoying a schoolgirlish naughtiness. One day the Committee was leaving Belfast (I think it was) by air. Seats had not been allocated, so the passengers crushed at the barrier in the usual way. We were in the open air, and the plane was about a hundred yards off, on the tarmac. Joyce and I and some others were near the front. There was also, right at the front too, a well-known B.B.C. commentator, very large. He knew Joyce, and they chatted awhile. Then she broke off and said to us, conspiratorially: 'There's going to be a mad scramble for seats. But I have a method. Collect some overcoats and hats for me.' We did, and as soon as the barrier lifted she was off like a shot, not a bit bothered about keeping up genteel appearances, straight across the bows of the B.B.C. man, who was anyway a bit disconcerted by a performance which belonged in, roughly, the same category as hitting your opponent's ankles with your hockey stick. When the rest of us reached the plane she was beckoning us from the front with the smile of a girl who'd just won the annual egg-and-spoon race at St Trinian's, by a ruse which wasn't altogether top-drawer but was indisputably funny and effective. Each spare coat and hat was draped over a good seat; no middles.

One tends to use school images when talking about her, and not only because she was herself a professional observer of schools of many kinds. There was a touch of the headmistress in her. A bit bossy, she used to describe herself. As I've said, she didn't want those she liked to have any markedly bad habits. By now, in 1980, I haven't smoked for more than a dozen years. But in the early sixties I did still smoke, chiefly a pipe. Joyce never failed to rebuke me for it, gently but firmly, until in the end, though I didn't at that period altogether stop smoking, I did generally lay off in her presence. If she had thought that any of us were drinking too much she would also, I have no doubt, have chided us persistently.

As to me, she was particularly sorry I couldn't be persuaded to become a Christian. After a year or two she seemed to have come to the decision that I was at least a Christian *manqué*, who would in all probability come round to recognising the rightness of the faith later on. So she kept me up to scratch on that possible future track, as the occasion arose. At a more homely level, she cared that we should all *look* right when we were on public parade. I have a habit, when a committee is really getting down to business, of kicking off my shoes. That she didn't at all care for, if those giving evidence could see what had happened. She wanted us all to be taken seriously by the witnesses, no matter how much we laughed at the behaviour of some of those witnesses once they'd gone. So, 'Richard dear, your shoes are off,' or 'Your tie is crooked again,' she'd say just before yet another entry by the heavy mob from the B.B.C. or I.T.A.

Soon after the Pilkington Report was published I wrote an essay, 'The Difficulties of Democratic Debate', about its extremely mixed and often violent reception, and sent Joyce a copy. I received the first of what was to become a seventeen-year-long sequence of neatly-handwritten, detailed responses to essays and books. She asked on that first occasion that, so far as possible, I send her everything I published, and I did. I am very sorry now that I did not preserve all those letters; they were always shrewd and often persuasive (our total failure to see eye-to-eye about class always excepted).

Later, we were members of the B.B.C.'s General Advisory Council at the same time; and my friend Roy Shaw, now Secretary General of the Arts Council, served at roughly the same period. It was interesting to see how Joyce usually sought us out, and liked to sit between us. I think she was showing solidarity with one well-defined way of thinking about broadcasting of which she approved. And if the balloon went up in the discussion she enjoyed being right in the middle of the argument.

It will be clear that she believed firmly in keeping friendships in good repair. The other day my wife came across a letter Joyce had written way back in the early 1960s, after her first visit to us. She stressed how important good friendships were to her – and went on to suggest that the two of them combine to continue to persuade me to stop smoking.

Out of many, two instances of the way she actively honoured her dues to friendship stand out for me. We spent the whole of the first half of the seventies in Paris, so our connections with

Joyce were by letter and card only. We came back to England in the spring of 1975 and sent out cards saying that we were now living in Farnham, about fifty miles south-west of London. Only a few days after we landed, the phone rang; that was still a fairly rare event. It was Joyce, to propose that she and Reggie motor down from Chelsea to welcome us back. A few days later they came to tea; a hundred-mile round trip simply to refresh a friendship.

The other instance is similar. In 1978, the year my wife and I both reached sixty, our children decided to throw a party in Farnham and invite all our friends and good acquaintances of the thirty-odd years since the war. We knew without doubt that Joyce and Reggie would make it in their way to come, and they did.

Now that she is dead, and we discover how many of us can claim her friendship, not just acquaintanceship, we realise far more how very well-developed and well-honed that capacity for friendship was. This is a rare and demanding gift. On her, it was happily exacting.

RICHARD GARNETT
AND TIM HELY-HUTCHINSON
A Very Satisfactory Author

RICHARD GARNETT: I was unpardonably late for my first appointment with Joyce Grenfell. She hated unpunctuality, and by the time I had arrived panting on the doorstep of her flat she had already rung my office and asked ominously, 'Is he *usually* unpunctual?' But once I was there she threw open a window high on the building, gave an instantly recognisable 'Yoo-hoo!' of welcome, and from this unpropitious beginning there developed as happy a relationship as ever editor had with author.

The Grenfells' flat, modest in size, but agreeably comfortable in character, seemed almost like a spring garden, with its fresh colours a pleasant contrast to the drab grey brick outside. The work always went on in her dining-room, a smallish room, with a magnificent dresser of plates on one wall and Mary Potter's portrait of Joyce in Marie Laurencin colours on another. The table was surrounded by elegant black and gold chairs, too good for everyday use, but getting it all the same. The green tablecloth would be strewn with typescript, parts of which had already been chopped up and reorganised by Reggie, who was always there, always helpful and to the point, giving the support of an amanuensis as well as a husband.

When Joyce thought of something new that she wanted to put in, she would first of all try it out for sound. Only when the rhythm – and often the accent – were right did she scribble it down, too hurriedly to be easily legible, but not too hastily for her to linger over changing a word that was still not right. It was slow, concentrated work, especially when three sets of galley proofs were snaking across the tablecloth. It would go on all morning, until we were boss-eyed with collating corrections, and Reggie and I were beginning to flag (Joyce did not like to catch herself flagging). Then we would sweep away the papers, and she would bring in a lunch of soup and cheese – excellent soup of her own making, and so compounded that the colour was as refreshing as the taste. Reggie would press a brimming glass of wine on me – Joyce didn't drink. And then she would relax, talk of friends old and new, and tell stories just a little earthier and more indiscreet than she liked to put in print. She was a great collector of the absurd, the pithy and the true.

Then it was back to business: checking facts, dates, spellings. The only uphill work was in trying to get her to describe her friends so that one could actually recognise them. I didn't doubt their golden qualities – but how did they talk, what did they look like? She was strangely reluctant to tell one. Yet if they had been imaginary friends – like old Hetty in her rocking-chair, or the Vice-Chancellor's Wife – she could have conjured them up in three words of monologue. There were drifts of photographs to be sorted through. She could be very glamorous on stage, but she never minded looking silly in a photograph. Her friends, however, must always be seen to advantage – not too many wrinkles. And then there was the index. Joyce and Reggie had never made an index in their lives. But they insisted on doing all the donkey-work. On my next visit it was all written out in Reggie's efficient angular writing. I had only to add a dash of expertise in sorting out a few tangles to be hailed as a genius and given all the credit – just the reverse of what usually happens.

For the book-jacket I wanted a photograph of Joyce looking friendly and brandishing an outsize invitation card – requesting the pleasure. Often the most obvious jacket is the most effective. Peter Letts took the photograph. His studio was new, well equipped with all that was strictly necessary, lights of all kinds, coloured backcloths, reflectors of various shapes, but nothing as yet in the way of 'reception' or creature comforts. In this brilliantly-lit hangar Joyce put on a performance for Peter and me as if we had been a full house. She sat on a very plain chair, holding the absurd card as if it were the most natural thing in the world, and once again she felt it important to get the sound right. As she went into each slightly varied pose, she greeted Peter with a convincing 'Hello!' of pleased surprise, as if the door had been unexpectedly opened by a series of old friends. Naturally he soon became one.

The appearance of the book was very important to her, and I was glad to be able to find her a binding material that was a fair match for the green tablecloth. And then, when it was well on its way, the time came to launch it to our salesmen at one of our quarterly sales conferences. Alan Maclean said a few words to the assembled reps, and in came Joyce in a smart green trouser suit and David Copperfield hat. 'What do you want me to say?' she asked in a whisper that everyone could hear. I thought she had settled all that, but one could hardly go wrong:

'Tell them how you first became an entertainer.'

She was away. It was beautifully done: impromptu, just enough of a performance to make it entertaining, but not to destroy the easy intimacy of a conversation among friends. They loved it. They loved her. Indeed it was the beginning of a love affair (on her part no less than ours) with the whole book trade.

She spoke at conferences and literary luncheons; she ranged the country with Jeremy Hadfield and Monica Cunningham, meeting booksellers, and enjoying each press, radio and television interview as if it were a new and unique experience. She visited our warehouse and made friends at the packing bench. And always there were signing sessions, up and down the country, and in Australia and South Africa as well. Signings can be a mechanical chore, but she had no patience with authors who let them seem so. Each time she signed a book it was a token of a friendly contact, however brief, between author and reader. She felt she had something of what she called 'nourishment' to offer her readers, just as she had done to men in hospitals during the war. And from the letters that her readers have written, it is clear that they felt the same.

Joyce did not speak of her private griefs. One of them was that she had no children. Perhaps that is why she felt such particular pleasure in producing her first book. It was something entirely of her own, and she loved it like a child.

TIM HELY-HUTCHINSON: Joyce's success in Australia with her first book was a publishing phenomenon. It started when a tape of Joyce at her London sales conference was played to the Australian sales force; recordings of previous English authors had often been howled down for their 'parochial' approach and jokey accents, but this one was different – they insisted on hearing it twice.

Joyce at first thought she was known in Australia principally through her tours there as an entertainer, and could rather easily be cajoled into singing a few bars of her song 'Ferryboats of Sydney'. In fact, the hundreds of people who queued up at signings nearly all talked about her films, which mattered least to her artistically, but which she began to praise as ambassadors. Once back in Australia she was her own best ambassador, with a remarkable schedule of engagements. She was, for instance, on thirteen full-length television shows in ten days.

Naturally, she became a connoisseur of interviewers; most of them became friends, but she occasionally applied her dictum about not liking to criticise but 'a little gentle mocking never did anyone any harm'. One television interviewer who was being petulant about his make-up had to suffer while an apparently oblivious Joyce sat next to him being fantastically nice to her own make-up girl and saying how little one needed if one had the right bones.

The publicity tour, which included every major Australian city, was punctuated with the comedies she endlessly noticed or engineered. Reggie played an important part in these perform-ances; I doubt, for example, if she would have ordered our taxi to stop for ten minutes because she wanted to watch a wedding (she was besotted with weddings) if not for the fun of provoking Reggie's dry, pleading assurances that this one was no different from any other she could watch another day. There was also, of course, the business of sending all the letters she wrote; one I received later was simply to remark that the maid in her hotel was called Shirlene.

However, it was Joyce's professionalism that most impressed those of us who worked with her in Australia. At her final engagement, a literary luncheon for four hundred, she spoke for half an hour without repeating any of the material she had used on the rest of her tour. When we exclaimed afterwards, she casually said it was to save us from being bored. She need not have worried.

HERBERT AXELL

In One of her Pleasant Places

It was one of Suffolk's magical June days, all wide blue sky over the Constable country marshes of the Royal Society for the Protection of Birds Minsmere bird reserve. We – Joyce, Reggie and I – were climbing the steps into the South Hide, from which I knew the view and the birds to be seen would be good. As usual, being with them, I was happy and felt their happiness too.

'Why,' Joyce asked me, 'are you humming that piece of *Coppelia*?'

'Oh, is that what it is?' I said. 'It seems to fit the day.'

In the tall, wooden hide, we swung our legs over the bench-seat and lifted up the viewing-flap. The incoming light showed agreement in Joyce's wonderful, serious little smile. A quick squeeze round my waist and she raised her binoculars to a pair of avocets throwing grasses at each other on a little island.

Bird reserves are made primarily for birds. More and more of these sites, however, especially those in pleasant places like Minsmere, well-stocked with wildlife and easily accessible, must also be made to cater for people. It is a splendid, necessary development. Birdwatching embraces every sort of person into a real fraternity of friendly people who, in their love affair with birds, wear their hearts on their sleeves. A bird reserve is the most honestly sociable place, where egalitarianism rules if only for the day; and for the resident warden and his wife it's a bit of heaven on earth. Our visitors, because they included people like the Grenfells, became as important to us, and as enjoyable, as our birds.

Joan and I first had the chance to fall in love with Joyce and Reggie in the early 1960s. Minsmere is only some half-hour's drive northwards from Snape Maltings, and they were among the many music-lovers, for whom a love of wildlife is also natural, who came to the reserve during the summer period of the Aldeburgh Music Festival. Their visits at first were rather short, between concerts or Joyce's rehearsals and usually with eminent friends, but later they came for longer periods. Then we could have lengthier discussions about the reserve's birds, its plants and its visitors.

Managing a bird reserve involves, to some extent, being in the entertainment industry, and it is good for the cause when visitors come across V.I.P.s. Joyce, like every professional, loved being recognised and played up nicely. But knowing that most very well-known people appreciate real time off, I soon suggested she and Reggie might come on days when we were closed, as well as on the open days. So, much to our benefit, we had them more often. The only little extra for which Joyce asked (typically not for herself) was that Benjamin Britten, a new R.S.P.B. member, infected by her enthusiasm I suspect, might be able to come over for a break in any rare free period that might unexpectedly occur for him at The Maltings. It was Joyce's idea, too, when her great friend and accompanist, Viola Tunnard, became so tragically paralysed that she might be brought over to watch birds here. By good fortune, we had begun to introduce wheelchair facilities in some of the hides at Minsmere, and, whenever they could, Jean and Christopher Cowan brought Viola from their house at Aldeburgh, where they were looking after her.

Relaxed and away from it all in lovely countryside, perfect strangers converse on sight. It was Joyce's delight to meet every kind of person, sometimes a dear little lady of eighty, moving slowly and stopping to look at new groups of flowers; or a wide-eyed child, out on his own for the very first time in the safety of a bird reserve; or an intense, hairy, rarity-chaser; mostly, though, lovely family parties. Joyce absorbed them all, and to their delight often stopped and talked to them. One day we saw what looked like a Red Indian ahead of us in the woods – all frilled leather, decorated head-band, hair to the shoulders, fierce face. For once, Joyce faltered in her tracks. Closing in on him, we could see he had a small pair of binoculars among the beads and bones around his neck, and when we spoke to him he replied in a voice that was soft and cultured English.

'What a lovely man!' said Joyce, when he had passed on. 'Doing his own thing. Do you get many like that?'

I said they were becoming a dying breed, but they used often to come in tribes, squaws and all, in old bangers, usually from one university.

Many times we had tea, *al fresco* on the sunny side of our cottage in the middle of the reserve – it always seemed to be sunny when they came, but, after all, it *was* mostly in June when dry, coastal Suffolk was at its driest. It was a real tea, with Joan's cakes and buns, and leisurely, too, if it was a closed day. Joyce would sing or practise a new piece of gentle mimicry, but never once did she try a version of a birdwatcher. To say it was a pity that such a person could not be included in her repertoire, much as we should all have loved it, would be greedy. Joyce gave us more than enough opportunity to laugh at ourselves in other guises.

In the early days, before the R.S.P.B. became rich and we were struggling to manipulate the earth, water and plants to induce more birds to breed and feed at Minsmere, we often discussed the U-turn which the British, still avid bird-killers in the early part of this century, had made. Joyce considered what might have brought out all the present compassion and loosened the purse strings to help with the conservation of wildlife. Was it reaction to the senselessness of destruction in war, of which, especially in her E.N.S.A. days, she had seen so much? Was it guilty conscience, and were we afraid now of having gone too far with urbanisation, toxic spraying, noisy and selfish use of every bit of countryside we could get to by car? In talking to many people in many places, Joyce did her bit for wildlife protection.

I said, 'A lot of this progress is due to communicators like you, Joyce, and Freddy Grisewood, Peter Scott, David Atten-borough, Robert Dougall. Radio, television and books have played the biggest part.'

Joyce knew a lot about birds, her senses being just as acutely tuned towards them as towards people, and was always asking questions which showed an out-of-the-ordinary humaneness. She was keenly interested in our special charges, hoping on each first visit in spring that the bitterns, marsh harriers, avocets, little terns and bearded tits, were off to a good start. She could always remember what success they had achieved in the previous year. Her interest in plants was somewhat greater. If it was a closed day, she would sometimes sit and draw them, doing it very well. She was easily the most observant visitor we ever had, and this was a delight, and it was inspiring.

A big odd-time task we had begun, which was to take years, was to make a mile-long road across the boggy marsh. The material we used was hoggin, sand and gravel deposited by the last glaciation, which we dug out of our heathland areas. A unit of the Royal Engineers did the most difficult section for us, a stretch of two hundred yards through wet reed-beds which required the laying and compacting of thousands of tons of hoggin before a weight-bearing road emerged. Joyce was in-trigued by the introduction of this ancient heathland gravel to marshland and was quick to notice when heather, gorse and other dry-land plants began to grow along the edge of the road. She wondered how long the seeds had remained dormant, buried on the heath. The light and space, let into what had been a dense bed of reeds, also allowed flowering wet-land plants – marsh orchid, yellow iris, hemp, agrimony, skullcap – to grow along the roadside. From year to year, Joyce noticed every new flower and how some had come and gone, their place having been taken over by taller, dominating species. Nobody else was so appreciative of these changes; she knew the climax vegetation along this piece of marshland road would be a marvellous mix-ture of sallows, alders, soft rush, birch, gorse and bramble, useful to insects and birds, and that is what it is now.

Above the marsh, at the edge of the path bordering a field of rye which, as she said, grew as high as an elephant's eye, we came across a mutual friend who was studying a patch of dove's-foot cranesbill. The plants, normally no more than four inches high on the poor soil of this higher ground, were exceptionally robust and the flowers were an unusually deep shade of pink. Perhaps some of the farmer's fertiliser had helped. Meeting a friend and an enthusiast, Joyce smiled widely, invitingly, arched eyebrows asking, 'What have you got?'

'Can it be a bloody cranesbill?' wondered our friend.

'No, dear, it ruddy can't be,' said Joyce, disdaining the obvious expletive. She knew *Geranium sanguineum* well enough from frequent visits, with Reggie or Viola, to that plant's proper limestone habitat in Cumbria.

In January 1970, she and Reggie, with other lovers of the Aldeburgh Festival, had the marvellous idea of trying to save the reed-beds behind the Maltings concert hall and turn them into a bird reserve. The sea, borne up the River Alde, had broken through the retaining embankment during storms in the previous September and the hundred acres of freshwater reed-marsh, rich with the variety of birds that this habitat can support, was in danger. The tides were enlarging the breaches in the wall twice every day, and the salt water would, in two or three decades, kill off the plants and turn this lovely Maltings back garden into a featureless sea of grey mud.

I was full of enthusiasm for the idea, picturing water-control devices that would maintain ponds, clumps of reeds and rushes, flowering water-plants, the odd group of willows and alders, with paths, benches and perhaps, a discreet, reed-thatched hide or two. What a lovely facility for patrons of The Maltings. I made a couple of surveys, one with Bill Roberts, River Authority area engineer and a Festival devotee, and while Reggie was in South Africa, reported via Joyce in London. If we could get the permission of the owner of the land, or buy it, the breaches could, I thought, be mended, but this must be done very quickly. Reggie wrote a long article in that season's Festival Programme, but the land could not be acquired, time passed, the sea water spoilt larger areas, and the project was lost. I never saw Joyce so disappointed as she was over this, but it was the only sad occasion, and we had many more years of happy days at Minsmere.

Three weeks before she died, at the end of November 1979, Joan and I went down to the Aldeburgh Bookshop where she was autographing copies of *In Pleasant Places*. This session had been postponed for a fortnight because of illness. There she was, straight-backed, smiling as widely as ever, the real professional – and drawing strength from Reggie at her side.

Patiently and with obvious pleasure, she inscribed every book more beautifully than any customer might have hoped for, and none was aware of her being in pain. While she was writing in a Christmas-present copy for my sister, a press photographer took a picture of us all that is one of our greatest treasures.

Trying to leave on a cheerful note, I said, 'Joyce, what I liked most in this book is your declaration that you live your life with zest.'

'So do you.'

We left the bookshop, not knowing we weren't to see her again. I was glowing. That was the Joyce we knew and would remember: always dispensing little bits of love to her friends.

MARGERY SHARP

Bon Comme le Pain

Dear Joyce!

I remember Joyce especially at Christmas. For many years my husband and I spent Christmas Day in Elm Park Gardens, and the beauty of it was that it was always the same – the same guests, the same tapestry of Christmas cards arranged by Reggie across the bookshelves, the same witty and beautiful place-cards painted by Joyce: for an essential part of Christmas is surely continuity. Thus though the flowers of her indoor garden might vary from year to year, there were always nosegays set out on the special circular table, usually very small ones, but each receiving as much individual attention as a florist's show-piece – probably more, for I do not think Joyce much cared for floral show-pieces: her taste was for the unpretending and unsophisticated. I once delighted her with a cutting of sweet geranium from off my kitchen windowsill, to be cherished to maturity in the sunshine of her smile.

Why be afraid of a cliché? Joyce wasn't. One of her great charms was that there was nothing precious about her. The material upon which she exercised her art was familiar to the point of banality, and if she transformed it into something rich and rare – huckaback into damask, a fat lady into a Spanish galleon – that was simply because nothing to her common was or mean. So let me say that Joyce was good as gold, *bon comme le pain*, kind as an angel and beloved by all who knew her.

> 'Had she no faults, then?' asks the poet.
> 'Yes, she has one, I must aver.
> When all the world conspires to praise her,
> The woman's deaf, and does not hear.'

But that wasn't Joyce. It was another endearing quality that she delighted in praise, as a proof of the delight she gave: there was a marvellous reciprocity between entertainer and entertained as she drew her listeners into a never unkind conspiracy to make fun. A tragedian may move to pity and terror, a satirist to heart-searching, but to move to laughter without bitterness is surely equally salutary to human nature in an age when fun is in short supply.

Dear Joyce!

ATHENE SEYLER

Spring Occasions

Joyce wrote to me when my husband died – 'Whenever I think of him, I smile, because he smiled.' And that is how I feel about Joyce, and I am sure everyone who met her shares this view of her. What fun she was! I look through the many letters I have from her, and there is a smile in so many of them. Two of them are little rhymed jingles thanking us for the spring lunches that we gave every year, a charming kind of thank-you letter and quite typical of her. Here is one:

> Your annual lunch is our delight.
> The sun is always shining bright
> But could not shine more brightly than
> Beloved Athene and her Man!
> The company is always good,
> So is the special hand-cooked food.
> Champagne – gardenias –
> Fish – fruit – veg,
> We thank for ALL
> Love – Joyce and Reg.

And another, after a luncheon when all the food served was pink or green, the colours of the Garrick Club tie:

> Ring the bells – fire the cannons
> Praises sing of both the Hannens.
> Praise the Garrick (lovely Club),
> Praise the rose and verdant grub.
> Every face a joy to see there
> All of us content to be there.
> Hail Athene, likewise Beau
> Hail to both – we love you so.

Blow the trumpet, beat the drum,
Thank you, loves, from your old chum
(and chum Reggie too)   Joyce.

Her letters were like seeing her in person with her gaiety and charm, and were vivid pictures of occasions. This one refers to a party where the button-holes we gave to the guests were camellias:

What a glorious party you gave us again this year. I think it was the best ever. I write with a camellia pinned to my bosom, and my head full of the pleasures of which we partook and experienced. You are darlings to do this for us and I hope you know just how much we appreciate it. Half the fun is familiarity – same nice people, same pretty room, Spring – it is an Occasion. And I must confess I look forward to seeing Daphne's hat every time. We were not let down this year, were we! A winner. Yours, on the other hand, was a *good* hat and very becoming.

She had drawn little pictures of us all on the menu, in our hats, which were a characteristically true comment on the manners of the period, 1959, when every lady wore a hat at luncheon. This was her gift of kindly caricature, which she showed so brilliantly on the stage in her sketches of people. What a descriptive pen she had. Here is another letter about one of the luncheons when all the button-holes were red roses:

The Annual event is one of our favourite functions – best hats and all. That room is a perfect setting. What with our rosy faces and rosy boutonnières and the great vase of roses in the middle of the table, it did really find us in the Pink.

How I wish that I could have written in the same vivid way to thank Joyce and Reggie every year for their perfect Boxing Day parties, which deserved far more appreciation than did our own efforts at luncheons. What a wonderful gift she had for Christmas decorations. The whole flat looked like a kind of Christmas tree, and the lovely little place-name cards with pictures of flowers, and the tiny babies' socks filled with sweetmeats by one's plate. Everything she did had an original twist –

even her acknowledgement, publicly, on a *Face the Music* programme, that she did not appreciate or know much about opera! This I found especially endearing, as I share her loss in this respect.

There is a nice typical phrase in one of her letters, in which she says that she and Reggie are to go to stay with friends, and she would rather not go '(Sh, Sh!)', for though she loves them she would rather be at home 'where I am familiar with the draughts'.

In another letter I find an intimate little reminder of her life and her likes and dislikes, oddly my own too. 'Wasn't the tennis splendid? but wearing.' This refers to a television recording of a match at Wimbledon – a novel way of describing the tension of watching first-class games. 'Do you watch soccer? Reggie and Gin are both avid fans, but I hate it – I prefer tennis.'

There is an interesting peep into her mind and methods of work in a letter from Cheltenham:

I am giving a talk at the Town Hall tonight. I was invited to give it a year ago and have spent the last week slogging over the wording of it, to be abandoned for notes on the night. Just to make sure of details this morning I read through the correspondence and discovered I had been asked to do a talk on *Music*! That was not what I had been slogging on all last week! But somehow I was fired by the new idea and glad of it. Coming down in the car I wrote out headings, and when I got here I had two and a half hours in which to sort them out, shape the thing, and now all I have to do is pray! I have salvaged some of the earlier work and woven it in. Interestingly enough I am rather glad of it because it is fresher than the other talk.

I have no record of her ever having any doubts about her ability to achieve what she had to do. If she had any, her Christian Science training would have made her able to overcome them, I think. The letter continues:

It is a poem of a day here. I receive at a luncheon in aid of the Distressed Gentlefolk of which Cheltenham has many! Reggie is the greatest support all through.

And, indeed, this last could be quoted at the end of everything that Joyce did or felt, and I am sure is the chief secret of her inspiration and success in everything she undertook in the fifty years of their marriage.

And so to the more serious side of her, which was perhaps the greater and overall part of her life. I have two letters showing this side of her. One when we were having to give up our Chelsea home, in which we had lived for fifty years, the house being pulled down to make room for a sub-power-station. She wrote:

Don't think we don't know what a wrench it must be. Mercifully life is eternal and these changes and problems will fade, and I find it comforting to begin to realise that Eternity is not acres and miles of nothingness, but actually continuity, day by day, of Life itself, wherever we are – S.W.3, or Norfolk, New York (ugh!) or Heaven.

Even here comes a little happy glint of laughter, in a typically constructive thought.

The other letter was written to me after my husband died and was a great solace to me, and helps me now in the loss of Joyce herself. She wrote:

I am so glad he is free from the limitations of the body and any distresses he has had to combat. He is all right, of course, and discovering the wonder that Life is continuity. It is you I feel for, darling, and I hope so much that very soon you will find that all the sad and difficult pictures that may haunt you now will somehow dissolve and you will find that Beau is restored to you as he was at his very best. You will know, I am sure, that useful prayer that says – 'Death is an horizon and an horizon is but the limitation of our view.'

That's it – 'the limitation of our view.' God's view never changes, and we are never, for the breath of an instant, out of that view, this side of death or the other.

So when I think of Joyce, I smile.

KATHARINE MOORE
A Pen-Friendship

In 1957 I heard Joyce quote Professor Raleigh's verse, 'I wish I loved the human race', and add: 'I do not know who this Professor Raleigh was but I should think he must have been a miserable misanthrope.' I ventured to write and tell her that she was mistaken, sending her two other poems of his to prove it. This brought me an immediate and characteristic reply: 'It was so nice of you to write as you did and I *love* both Raleigh poems. I'd no idea. I love him from now on.'

This was the beginning of our pen-friendship which continued until her death. For me it was a completely magical bonus. I rather suspect that she made everyone feel that they were of importance to her, however improbable this seemed, but I never ceased to marvel at the time and trouble she spent on someone who had not the slightest claim upon her.

Our letters very soon plunged into all sorts of topics – in fact the second was on the relation of time to eternity, and this led on to Traherne's poetry. Traherne seems to me to have much in common with Joyce. Neither ever took joy in life for granted or forgot to savour it. Her letters are full of joy in nature, books, music, places, people and work. I think of Shakespeare's line about Beatrice, 'There was a star danced, and under that was I born.' Here are just a very few of the many varied joyful passages in the letters:

6 days silence in lovely Cumberland, curlew calls, cold winds but blue patches, wild roses and water fit to drink.

Can you think of anything pleasanter than doing a job you enjoy and on top of that making such a fat sum for some very good causes.

May I say thank you – for the lovely Christopher Smart poem 'Stupendous Stranger' – what a joy! And 'Mosaic Thorn'. It's so *exact*, it makes you gasp with pleasure.

Isn't it odd the way people get sad about happy times in the past just because they are past: I go *on* enjoying them.

Joyce also had the art of communicating her joys so vividly in her letters that I could share them and in return she shared mine, and her response, appreciative and humorous, enhanced them. I used to send her anecdotes about my grandchildren, secure in her sympathetic enjoyment where others might well have been bored. There was this characteristic comment on a five-year-old's outburst: 'My life is a bane unless I have a purpill velvit dress' – 'What a sense of drama, what a passionate heart. I have no taste for purpill, but if I did it would have to be velvit.'

She was the perfect correspondent, always answering letters properly, continuing a line of argument or a discussion before embarking on fresh experiences. She also had a habit of setting the scene which added to the vividness and immediacy of the communication:

I write from an attic in an orange sandstone house, a blackbird is making most lovely wet notes.

or again:

Today is like Thomas Hardy's 'Spectre grey frost, the weakening eye of day lost in a desolate sky.' Roughly that's how it is in London. I'm consoled by the charm of a little bobble fringe, now sooty black, in the plane tree outside my window.

She must have written letters almost as easily and naturally as breathing, and they were dashed off from all sorts of places and in all sorts of situations – at Euston Station, from trains, from planes, in the midst of packing, punctuated by incessant phone calls. In a life as full as hers time was so precious, and yet she never seemed to be the slave of time nor gave the impression that letter-writing was a burden and she must have had an enormous correspondence always awaiting her.

It's like being given a present to be given two free hours. In it I've already swept and dusted the flat and laid the supper and now I have a little while left so I can write to you.

It never failed to astonish me that though the busiest, she was also the promptest to answer letters. We both appreciated quick response, and our correspondence was like bursts of conversation occurring about four to six times in a year. Her letters were seldom short, the longest filling eight large foolscap pages of small writing and ranging over an extraordinary variety of subjects: the society, culture and scenery, flowers and birds of Australia, New Zealand, Hong Kong, Singapore and South Africa, including unforgettably vivid descriptions, a discussion on 'responsibility' (with reference to an article by John Wain), on the Institute of Race Relations, on the writing of poetry, on education, an account of a controversial film and of a theatrical production at the Old Vic, anecdotes about children, about clothes and shopping, and finally a passage describing most movingly the death of an old friend.

I *know* as I sat with her that her essence, her live being was absolutely unchanged, whole and eternal.

In the middle of this mammoth letter she remarks, 'Heavens, this is turning into a book!' and at the end: 'If there was ever a self-indulgent correspondent, this is one.' My view was just the opposite – it was indulgent all right, but to the recipient. Yet whatever riches her generosity bestowed, there was never the least sense of patronage. She was endlessly encouraging about my writing, but also by asking for advice about hers and sending me her poems and discussing her broadcasts she managed to give me, at any rate, a sense of some sort of exchange, though I always wished I could think of anything I could really do for her in return for the enormous pleasure her letters gave me, and something more than pleasure.

The two years from 1972 to 1974 were bad ones for me as during them I lost my husband, my closest friend, and a dear stepdaughter and niece. Joyce's letters during that time were a source of comfort and power.

She had a certainty that love is immortal, that 'Death is only a horizon, that "all is well".'

God *is* Life, Truth and Love. Perhaps one should start with God is Truth and Love and they are Life. I think that is better.

Her strong faith and courage shone, and still shine out in the darkness. She is one of those of whom the poet Vaughan wrote:

They are our beacon fires.

JOSEPH MCCULLOCH

Joyce in Dialogue

When we restored St Mary-le-Bow, which Hitler's bombs had devastated in 1941, we put in twin pulpits, one each side of the church, so that two people could face each other, and converse naturally and informally across the intervening space, before an audience of mainly City people. The church was reconsecrated in 1964, and from the first these Tuesday lunch-hour dialogues became very popular. The building was always full to overcrowding, not least because the occupants of what came to be known as the visitor's pulpit were men and women of distinction and fame in various professions and very much the sort of people whom everybody wanted both to see and hear. Before very long the dialogues had become a kind of institution in the life of the City. The topics discussed were live, in the sense that they raised issues very much alive in people's minds. The home pulpit was usually occupied by me, whose role was to act as interlocutor, though sometimes I paired off the distinguished visitors to engage with each other in a sharing of minds. The aim of these public conversations was not controversy so much as a free interchange of ideas on a chosen topic, an occasion to question assumptions and make up one's mind in which direction the truth of the matter lay.

Joyce was very much in favour of the project from the start, but the City had to wait until January 1967 before professional engagements allowed her to occupy for the first time what was by then a very well-known platform. She has written about this experience in the second volume of her autobiography, *In Pleasant Places*:

I must say that I felt a particular sense of privilege whenever I was one of the occupants of the second pulpit. At first I wasn't sure how to approach the dialogue. Not as a preacher, that was certain. So why was I up there, with a microphone hung round my neck and a velvet cushion to lean on if I felt like it, and forty minutes of discussion time lying ahead? I decided I was there to share my findings of ways that work in my daily doings and relationships; and, out of a sense of gratitude and wonder, to bear witness to my increasing certainty – that is central to the way I try to live my life – of the power of God.

I can never forget that first public dialogue with Joyce, nor, I am sure, can the many who listened to it, spellbound. From the outset, it was unusual. As we came into the church, the whole overcrowded expectant audience of City workers, from directors to clerks and typists, rose to her with tremendous applause, as though greeting a personal friend too long awaited. In the other pulpit, she was, as ever, herself: spontaneous, direct, unaffected, but always shrewd and penetrating. After that first dialogue, it was taken for granted by both of us that the freedom of the pulpit was hers. She came every year, sometimes more than once, and the City's welcome was always the same thunderous greeting of appreciation and delight.

In 1974 we published a selection of twenty of the dialogues in a book entitled *Under Bow Bells*. I prefaced the dialogue which the publishers had chosen from what, by then, was a collection of Joyce's pulpit conversations, in an attempt to describe her as not only the City audiences knew her but also as she was known wherever she went.

As she came into the church, the crowded audience erupted into a spontaneous applause of welcome. If ever there was anyone with whom they felt in personal *rapport*, it was certainly she, the communicator *par excellence*. Whether the people with her are two or three gathered together, or thousands, or indeed millions, she is the same radiant person, spontaneous, free, aware and very much alive, exceptionally gifted and utterly sincere, serious and humorous, swift in sympathy, a brilliant mimic and comedienne; above all, a fundamentally happy woman. What she communicates in any medium is an unusual understanding of our common humanity, completely devoid of malice and all uncharitableness. Joyce Grenfell can expose our comic crassness – and yet more our tragic stupidity – and leave us somehow feeling that behind it all the universe is not against us.

To describe her professionally merely as an actress is a considerable understatement. She is chiefly famous as a *diseuse*, writing all her own material for her character sketches and songs. One of the happiest evenings at the theatre or on television is when Joyce is the sole performer, and you are taken through an enchanting variety of her adroit impressions of characters both comic and pathetic, magically peopling the stage with *dramatis personae* who exist only in her imagination and yours. Tall, commanding in stage presence, graceful in movement, she can yet become a waif, a duchess, a harassed school-teacher, what you will.

Her personal friends know her as one who enjoys a happy married life, not far off its golden anniversary, and as a phenomenally hard worker who still has time to give to others her hospitality and to share theirs. Basically she is serious-minded, as her published writings often reveal. It is because she sees that life for many people is a hard grind that she has worked to lighten it with her gift of laughter.

For my wife and myself every Tuesday was 'dialogue day' and an enjoyable event. But our hearts were never more gladdened with happy anticipation than when it was Joyce who was coming. At noon (she was always punctual) she ascended the stairs, and we sat down to swap news and enjoy an hour's togetherness before we had to face the dialogue, climb our pulpit stairs, and draw so many City friends into our conversation. Perhaps the best dialogues she gave us, some of which were televised, were those Tuesdays before Christmas. They were certainly a wonderful preparation for a festival of light.

The dialogue which was published in *Under Bow Bells* was probably chosen because its topic was particularly revealing of Joyce herself. It was about being alive and what makes people alive. The opening of that conversation is very much worth repeating here. I had asked Joyce as a person I knew to be extraordinarily full of life, what it is that makes people really come to life:

JOYCE: Well, for me, I think it is expressing what I understand God to be. If you ask, 'What is Life?', I suppose life is the presence of God. I think that people are lively – I don't mean a euphoric, hysterical way, but in the sense of being aware – because they are more conscious of that which truly *is*.

I remember years ago being invited to do a part in a series on radio. *Wishes for a Godchild* was the subject, and I began to think about it and found that the thing I would wish for anybody I loved would be the possibility of never coming to the end of discovery. I think it is what makes life worth living. I think what one wants to discover is what life is for, what is real, what you can depend on, what never changes, and that you yourself should be changeable enough to let go of the things that have no real value. Mark you, I didn't do that when I was very young.

J.MCC: Were you looking for Joyce Grenfell?

JOYCE: No, I don't think so. I think I knew her! No, actually I think what I was doing, what I am doing now, is *losing* Joyce Grenfell, or hoping to, and finding out – this sounds very solemn, but I think this is the right place to say it – finding out the person God made. The older you get the more you realise that happiness is losing your false sense of what you are, your *false self*. What was that lovely quotation you told me upstairs just now? Goethe, was it?

J.MCC: 'Become what you are!'

JOYCE: 'Become what you are.' Well that, interpreted, means become what your true potential is, your spiritual wholeness.

Joyce could talk like that to City gents in their black coats and striped trousers and to typists in their pretty frocks, and they took her to their hearts.

There were many things she said on those unforgettable Tuesdays which I doubt if anybody else could have said without various modifying 'ifs' and 'buts'. She was always unequivocally downright: she said what she meant, and she meant what she said. Hence she could talk of eternal values and human frailties with equal directness. As the years went on, her influence on many in the City grew. One of them, after Joyce had been the visitor in the pulpit, said darkly to me, as though I might not agree with him, 'That was more effective than a hundred sermons.' And yet she was no sermonising moralist or pulpiteer. I was more than content that she was just the right person to get certain things said which carried the kind of truth people were seeking. To quote again from her dialogue: 'The problem today is that there is apparently so much freedom that people don't know where they are: they are dizzy with freedom.'

When I said how aptly that phrase describes our age, Joyce answered, 'Yes, I've never thought of it before. But, Joseph, the interesting thing is that we make our own prison walls, don't we?'

Dear Joyce. Many in the City of London miss her. They were hungry sheep that looked up and were fed. What was her secret? I think it was somewhere to be found in a quotation we both cherished: 'What can sadden those who serve the everlasting joy?'

JOYCE GRENFELL

Wishes for a Godchild

I think one of the top compliments you can be given is to be asked by friends you love to be a godparent to their child. (I know there are 'worldly' reasons for asking people to be god-parents but I am talking about the unworldly kind of invitation when love is the real reason.)

Of course when one loves one's church one wants to help it, but for many years now I have not felt able to be an official godparent because of the vows a godparent is called upon to make. In all humility, I just cannot believe that a child is only acceptable to God when he has been baptised.

I believe that a child of God is, and always has been and always will be, a spiritual identity. He doesn't have to be baptised, or die, to become spiritual. Spirituality is his birth-right, as I see it, and nothing can alter this.

So although I don't feel able to be an official godmother, I am an unofficial one, who cares very much about the children she is particularly invited to love and cherish; and the first wish I wish my unofficial godchild is a sort of blessed curiosity that leads to discovery – on all levels.

Discovery of nature: of flowers, of birds and beasts. (Just think of the design of a fern, a shell, a petal, a feather; of moss and frost patterns!) Then there is the discovery of sound, of music – *all* kinds of music; music for moving to, music for sitting still and listening to and, if possible, music for taking part in. And the discovery of words and using them; of poetry and reading. Of course, reading is one of the best ways to discovery – dis-covery of the vastness and the variety of creation.

Then I wish my godchild the discovery of the possibility of

love and friendship that in turn lead to the joy of sharing; and of giving acceptance with generosity and grace. And above all the discovery of the light that shines in all these things and these ideas and brings them into focus – the light of the discovery of that which is real, never changing and yet continuously new – and that is, our spiritual understanding.

I wish that my godchild may have enthusiasm, because the kind of enthusiasm I mean not only has no place in it for boredom, but it adds quality to every experience and is attractive and infectious. I don't mean narrow, fanatical enthusiasms. I mean joy of living; the expectancy of good, because optimism, as I see it, is faith in the certainty that good is all powerful; and good is always there to be discovered, in people and, therefore, in situations and circumstances.

In Ecclesiastes it says: 'God made man upright, but they have sought out many inventions.' I think 'they' means those of us who believe they are out on their own struggling to make sense of our mixed up ideas of what life is.

I wish my godchild the discovery that teaches him he is, as God made him, 'upright'; in other words, spiritually whole, never on his own but always inseparable from the source of his true being.

In earthly terms I wish him something that sounds contradictory after saying he is never on his own, because I wish he might be taught to be – in the human sense – able to be alone, quietly, on his own for some part of every day so that, more and more, as he grows up, he can discover that he is, in the spiritual sense, never alone at all.

And I wish him a sense of proportion, because that is what I think a sense of humour is; and, to repeat, I wish him an endless sense of discovery and delight in all things that are true, a sense of real values, a sense of grateful wonder – and God bless him.

LEONARD GERSHE
The Letter

I was privileged to enjoy thirty-two years of uninterrupted friendship with Joyce – uninterrupted because Joyce was an avid and prolific correspondent. When we were not together (I live in California), letters flew back and forth between us at least once a week and sometimes there were two or even three letters in one week. One letter in particular was a remarkable piece of writing which enriched my life and helped me through a difficult time. This letter from Joyce arrived some days after the death of a very dear friend, Flobe (Mrs Shirley) Burden. Flobe was my first loved friend to die, and her death was sudden, surprising and shocking. It was a traumatic loss for me, and for days I went around in a gloomy haze of depression, anger and self-pity. Then Joyce's letter arrived, and it opened up for me a whole new way of thinking about death and how to deal with it. Since Flobe's death, I have suffered other severe losses and I have always turned to the wisdom in Joyce's letter which has never failed to comfort me.

With Joyce's permission I have shared this letter with others seeking the same help I needed. All of them have thanked me profusely and have acknowledged the fact that it did, in fact, enlighten them and help them through some of their darkest moments. I am certain that Joyce would have no objection to my sharing this letter now with you, the reader.

January 11th 1969

Darling Leonard:

I am so saddened by your news of Flobe's death. I know just how much she meant to you. I send you immediate and loving thoughts. Believing as I do that man is spiritual here and now *wherever* he may

185

seem to be, I have no doubts that Flobe is simply continuing in the continuity of life: and, that is, in the spiritual realm where she has always essentially been. We think we love someone for their looks; their walk maybe; tone of voice, touch – but when you analyse it it is really for their qualities – their warmth, their humour, their intelligence, kindness, etc. These things are spiritual qualities and are recognisable only by the spiritual in us. This, to me, is proof of spirituality. We may think it's the shape of a person's nose or the way the eyes light up or whatever it is, but in fact it is the *impression* these things have on us and this is not physical or material, is it? So, although the sense of loss is brutal and a shock – when you can look at it and think of it and feel the very real gratitude you have for having known and loved someone, then I think a sense of *real* reality takes over and one comes to the reasonable conclusion that spirituality is a reality; a continuing reality of all-good.

It is tough on Shirley and on you and on all who love her, but I believe the way to peace is not to mourn, but to free her in your mind and heart and realise she is always whole, always real because she is spiritual – *and so are you.*

We don't become spiritual *when* we die. We have always been spiritual and that, as I see it, is what life is for – to discover and rejoice in this. It leads into harmonious living *now*. It reveals what is actually *real* and *durable.*

Darling, I wish we were where we could talk. I know what Flobe means to you and I rejoice for all the good she brought into your life. Nothing can touch this. Shirley will be all right, I'm sure, once he is over this horrid shock – because when you have known real happiness, it is a part of your very being and nothing touches that, either – but, of course, it must be acknowledged as real.

Do you remember a quotation I wrote to you when your father went? I find it so good and so true: 'Death is an horizon – and an horizon is only the limitation of our view.'

I send you much love.

Joyce

JOYCE GRENFELL
My Way of Prayer

'Pray without ceasing,' it says in the Bible. What does that mean? Get down on your knees and stay there? Not as I see it. What is praying, and need we kneel to do it? For me prayer is not petitioning, not asking God to change anything; it is grateful acknowledgement of all the good God has already done, continues to do and continues to be; and in finding the place (the consciousness) where experience of His limitless provision of good is reality.

I believe this reality is where His children, you and I, spiritually made 'in His image and likeness' already belong. The human 'me', with my limited sense and frailty, is not this image, but the spiritual likeness is the true identity of each one of us, and prayer is acknowledgement of this likeness; and of our inseparability from God.

Why do I pray? To be aware of what God has ordained, made perfect, and is carrying out. Praying is being open to the power of His love, His truth and His life. Jesus is the Way, and His teaching says, 'There is none good but one, that is God.' 'I can of myself do nothing.' Nor can we.

Paul says, 'the natural man receiveth not the things of the Spirit of God: for they are foolishness unto him; neither can he know them because they are spiritually discerned.' This spiritual discernment (understanding) is ours *now* and can be used.

I find as I try to acknowledge, through spiritual discernment, what God has already done, I find answers to problems. This kind of praying is done wherever I happen to be, on or off my knees, day or night, in a bus, a bath, in crowds or alone.

I think what I mean by discernment is illustrated in this

anecdote: a small boy was asked: 'What do you think God is?' He paused before he answered. 'God isn't a think; He's a feel.'

One of my favourite commands in the Bible is 'Be still and know that I am God.' It does not tell us to be still and hope; it says be still and *know*. A comforting certainty lies behind that command; it *is* possible.

There is a great hunger, perhaps as never before, for a sense of reliable harmony in a world where the opposite is so noisily and cruelly evident. And that is putting it mildly. I find it is a practical help in any situation, and not only for myself, to realise and be able to feel that God's harmony is *always* going on even when it appears to be hidden by our mistaken, limited view and the material evidence to the contrary.

Thus prayer, for me, is acknowledging (not as whistling in the dark but as realistic understanding) the unfluctuating presence of God's harmony. It helps me to find an actual sense of what spiritual reality is; 'the kingdom of heaven is at hand'. Not a think but a feel.

Where do good ideas come from? I believe they are direct awareness of the provision of God's wisdom and power acknowledged and accepted.

I was once stuck in a lift. My companion, terrified, turned pale and looked desperate. I don't much like being stuck in lifts either, but my overwhelming desire at that moment was to relieve her great fear, and, as you may have noticed, when someone else is afraid it can make one braver. I said: 'Wherever we are, we are always in the same place – whether we are in a lift, on or under ground, in the air, on or in the sea, in or out of buildings.' By which I meant that as the spiritual child of God one can never, for a fraction of a second, be outside His encompassing Love.

The lift moved, came down, and we went on our ways. Some years later I met the same girl, and she thanked me for what I'd said that day in the lift. She had found it useful ever since. 'What *did* I say?' I asked, for I had no recollection of it. 'Wherever we are we are always in the same place.'

I knew God had not singled me out to receive a good idea when it was needed, for His supply of good ideas is infinite and always available to everyone. That day in the lift one was needed, and it was supplied and shared. Prayer (my desire to help) was answered in acknowledgement of God's unending love. I believe all good ideas, and indeed all good in whatever form it appears, is evidence of God's ever presence.

This way of prayer for me is the only way to find guidance, health, harmony in all its various manifestations such as good relationships, employment, supply, etc. As I began by saying, I pray by trying to acknowledge the fact of God's total, continuing provision of all good; and that each one of us as His spiritual likeness reflects this goodness.

Prayer is also learning, and practising, to replace a lonely sense of separation, of struggling on our own, being afraid, inadequate and doubtful, with the home-coming sense of belonging as the beloved child of God, who is all good. This is reality, God's reality.

GEOFFREY HOWARD WHITE

The Address

given at the Service of Thanksgiving
for the life of Joyce Grenfell
in Westminster Abbey, 7 February 1980

St Matthew's Gospel, Chapter 25, Verse 15: 'And to one he gave five talents, to another two, and to another one.'

The cover of Joyce Grenfell's book, *In Pleasant Places*, shows a view of my former Cumbrian parish, which she first visited in 1946. Return visits were made with Reggie, her husband, once or twice a year, until last mid-September. They made many friends in the valley, visited them regularly and came to the village church, where to our delight Joyce sang her own descants in the hymns.

God gave talents generously when Joyce was born – she knew they came from God and worked hard to develop them. So it was that, alone on the stage, or with the help of a pianist friend, Joyce could make us laugh, cry and laugh again – all without one cruel, unkind or unclean word or thought. Her books are bestsellers, her convictions there for all to read.

You may not know that in 1977 Joyce spoke from where I now stand. This is how she summarised what she said from this pulpit: 'My talk was on the recurring theme that continues to run through my own explorations, the discovery of that which is good, therefore eternal, therefore changeless and present now.'

The Dean in his letter to me wrote, 'We at Westminster

Abbey owe a lot to Joyce.' The same can be said about Rosehill Theatre in Cumbria. Joyce was a trustee and appeared for four nights, without fee, to the usual full houses, to raise money for the Trustee Fund.

She could draw, paint, compose; her records will be played, her films remembered – and she was a joy to see and hear on *Face the Music*. She was a member of the Pilkington Committee, and of the Churchill Memorial Foundation, and President of the Society of Women Writers and Journalists. There surely we have a remarkable result of the use of God-given talents.

Joyce and Reggie were within twelve days of their Golden Wedding. They had kept the Prayer Book promise to 'love and to cherish ... and keep only to each other ... till death us do part.'

She retained throughout life the wonder of a child at the sight of a wild flower, a bird, or badgers playing in the twilight.

I can tell of another talent Joyce developed. It is one which God gives to each one of us. Her close friends will know what I am going to say. Richard Baker knows, as was shown by his sincere tribute on the Television news and his article in the *Observer*. Bernard Levin and Clive James know, as was shown by their articles in the *Sunday Times* and *Observer*.

Before I tell you what it is, please forgive a personal reference to show my authority for what I am going to say. From sixteen to twenty-four years of age I trained for Ordination at the Mother House of the Society of the Sacred Mission. As students we lived the same life as the monks. To this monastery came clergy of all ranks, leading theologians, monks on holiday, monks from other monasteries, missionaries and many lay Christians. In my country parish I inherited, from former Vicars, parishioners with a solid, simple faith. I have watched that faith working out in the crises of life and gained much from the experience. I have served under six Diocesan Bishops. One Archbishop and eighteen Bishops have worshipped in my village church. I have listened to, and talked with, most of the people mentioned regarding the Christian faith, its implications and practice. There is my authority to underline what I am going to say.

The simple truth is, Joyce Grenfell was the most spiritually-minded person I have ever met.

She spent one hour each day with her Bible and with what she called her 'Holy Books', and took what she learned from God in that hour into her very busy day.

This is the other talent – given to us all – used by Joyce: the power to learn of God, to know Him, to be known by Him – and to be guided by His Holy Spirit.

She strove to heal every breach between people she came across and kept the Biblical Commandment: 'Thou shalt love the Lord thy God, with all thy heart, with all thy soul, with all thy strength and with all thy mind ... and thy neighbour as thyself.'

Joyce did just that: and I claim that is why, with the use of her other talents, she became the Joyce Grenfell we knew and loved so well.

Some have thought she had no difficulties or problems. She had her share.

Thinking of this part of her life the following words of Our Lord come to mind: 'Therefore whosoever heareth these sayings of mine, and doeth them, I will liken him unto a wise man, which built his house upon a rock. And the rain descended, and the floods came, and the winds blew, and beat upon that house; and it fell not: for it was founded upon a rock.'

So it was with Joyce. That rock was her faith in God, and the teaching of Jesus Christ.

So as we take our part in this service, remembering the life of Joyce Grenfell, I have, as you have, many happy memories. My greatest, and most abiding, will be that I have known about her deep, unshakeable faith in God, and of her search for things eternal and true.

May God grant that my chance of heaven could be one hundredth the part of hers.

I am confident, that as she came into the nearer presence of

God, some other words from the parable of the talents could be heard: 'Well done, thou good and faithful servant ... enter thou into the joy of thy Lord.'

May she rest in peace.

NOTE

The music for the Service was arranged by Joseph Cooper in collaboration with Douglas Guest, Organist and Master of the Choristers of Westminster Abbey. Before the Service Mozart's *Eine kleine Nachtmusik* and Bach's *Sheep may safely graze* were played by the Royal College of Music Chamber Orchestra conducted by Sir David Willcocks. During the Service Douglas Guest conducted the Choir in an early Anthem of Britten's *Of one that is so fair and bright*, and also *O Clap your hands* by Vaughan Williams. After the Service Bach's Toccata and Fugue in D minor was played by Christopher Herrick, Sub-Organist of Westminster Abbey.

The Bidding

Spoken by the Dean of Westminster
at the Service of Thanksgiving

We are gathered here today to give thanks to God for the life of Joyce Grenfell.

We thank Him.

For her love of people: for the friendship she gave (and fostered with letters) to so many friends all over the world:

For her invariable expectancy of good and the enthusiasm with which she greeted every day:

For the quickness of her perception; and for her gift of communication:

For her hatred of cruelty, and the gentleness with which she exercised her art:

For the inspiration and joy she found in her long marriage:

For her laughter:

For her endless delight in discovery, and her genuine love of simplicity:

For her love of words; of every kind of music; of colour, and of form:

For her love of flowers; particularly wild flowers: and of birds:

For her deep devotion to things of the spirit; her faithfulness in adversity; her tolerance, and her courage:

For her beauty:

And above all for the great generosity of her heart, and her love of that which is good.

Thanks be to God.

Index